THE NAMES OF GOD

How to Pray with God's Names

CAROLINE BIMBO AFOLALU

Copyright © 2022 Caroline Bimbo Afolalu

All rights reserved

No part of this book can be reproduced in any form or by written electronic or mechanical, including photocopying, recording, or by any information retrieval system without written permission in writing by the author

Published by
Whitstone Books
Croydon UK
March 2022

Printed in Great Britain

Although every precaution has been taken in the preparation of this book, the publisher and author assume no responsibility for errors or omissions. Neither is any liability assumed for damages resulting from the use of the information held herein.

ISBN 978-0-9574755-5-7

THE NAMES OF GOD

How to Pray with God's Names

"The Name of the Lord is a strong tower; the righteous man runs into it and is safe."
Proverbs 18:10

CONTENTS

Dedication xi
Acknowledgements xiii
Introduction xv
   The Lord's Prayer xviii

Chapter 1   El Shaddai - The Almighty God 1

Chapter 2   Jehovah Chereb - The Lord Our Sword 6

Chapter 3   Jehovah Sabaoth - The Lord of Hosts 9

Chapter 4   El Hannum - The Gracious God 12

Chapter 5   El Elyon - The Most-High God 15

Chapter 6   Elohim Bashamayim - The God in Heaven 18
   The Prayer of King Jehoshaphat 19

Chapter 7   Elohim Kedoshim - The Holy God 22

Chapter 8   El Emeth - The God of Truth 26

Chapter 9   Elohim Yeshuati - God of Our Salvation 30

Chapter 10 El Gibbor - The Mighty God 33
   The Prayer of Jeremiah 34
   God's Response to Jeremiah's Prayer 36

Chapter 11 El Gemuah - The God of Recompense 37

Chapter 12 Jehovah Bore - The Lord the Creator 39

Chapter 13 Elohim Chayim - The Living God 41
   The Prayer of Elijah 43

Chapter 14 Jehovah Maginnenu - The Lord Our Defence 45
   Apostle Paul's Spiritual Warfare Strategies 46
   A Psalm of David 47

Chapter 15 El Hakkabod - The God of Glory 49

Chapter 16 Jehovah Jireh - The Lord Shall Provide 52

Chapter 17 El Roi - The God Who Sees 55

Chapter 18 El Emunah - The Faithful God 58

Chapter 19 Jehovah Ori - The Lord Our Light 60

Chapter 20 Jehovah Goelekh - The Lord Our Redeemer 65
   The Concept of Born Again 67

Chapter 21 Elohim Macheslanu - God Our Refuge 69
   Psalm 91 70

Chapter 22 El Meleki - God Our King 72
   A Psalm of Praise of David 74

Chapter 23 EL Nekamoth - The God Who Avenges 75

Chapter 24 Jehovah Selai - The Lord Our Rock 78

Chapter 25 Elohim Azar - God Our Helper 81

Chapter 26 Jehovah Nissi - The Lord Our Banner 83

Chapter 27 Jehovah Rapha - The Lord Who Heals 85
   The Prayer of John for Health and Prosperity 86

Chapter 28 Emmanuel - God is With Us 88

Chapter 29 El Olam - The Everlasting God 91

Chapter 30 Jehovah Eloheeka - The Lord Our God 94

Chapter 31 Jehovah Maozi - The Lord Our Strength 96
   The Prayer of Samson for Strength 97

Chapter 32 Jehovah Eloheenu - The Lord Our God 99

Chapter 33 Jehovah Hoseenu - The Lord Our Maker 101

Chapter 34 Jehovah Shalom - The Lord Our Peace 104

Chapter 35 Jehovah Yisrael - The God of Israel 108

Chapter 36 Jehovah Shammah - The Lord is There 110

Chapter 37 I AM - I AM Who I AM 114

Chapter 38 Jehovah Tsidkenu - The Lord Our Righteousness .. 116

Chapter 39 Jehovah Shaphat - The Lord Our Judge.................. 119

Chapter 40 El Rachum - The Merciful God................................ 121
   The Prayer of Jonah against God's Compassion:...................... 124
   God's Response to Jonah's Prayer and Complaints................... 125
   Abraham's intercession for Sodom and Gomorrah................... 127
   Moses' intercession for the Israelites 128

Chapter 41 Elohim Avraham, Yitzhak V Yaakov - The God of
            Abraham, Isaac, and Jacob 130

Chapter 42 Jehovah Mekaddishkem - The Lord Who Sanctifies
            133

Chapter 43 Elohim - The Lord God 137

Chapter 44 Jehovah Rohi - The Lord Our Shepherd 139
   Psalm 23.. 140
   Jesus the Good Shepherd 142

Chapter 45 Jehovah Misgab - The Lord Our High Tower......... 144

Chapter 46 Adonai - The Lord God 148

Chapter 47 El Nas - The Forgiving God 151

Chapter 48 Jehovah Makkeh - The Lord Who Smites................ 154

Chapter 49 El Kanna - The Jealous God..................................... 158

Chapter 50 Yahweh - The Lord 164

Chapter 51　Jehovah - The Lord 166

Chapter 52　El Ashiyb - The Lord Our Restorer 168

Chapter 53　Jehovah Pelet - The Lord Our Deliverer 175
   Prayer for Deliverance (Writer's Version) 178
   David's Song of Praise and Deliverance 180

Chapter 54　El Achba - The Lord Who Hides 184
   David's Prayer of Repentance 186
   Persistent Prayer Request 188

Chapter 55　Jah - Jehovah 191

Chapter 56　Jehovah Magowr - The Fountain of Living Water .. 193

Chapter 57　Yeshua - The Lord of Salvation 197

Chapter 58　Messiah - Christ the Anointed One 201

Chapter 59　Jesus - Saviour 204

Chapter 60　Other Names and Title of Jesus 207
   Son of Man 207
   Son of God 208
   Christ 209
   The Mediator 210
   High Priest 210
   The Way 211
   Lamb of God 211
   Lion of Judah 211
   Alpha and Omega 212
   Bright and Morning Star 213
   The Root of David 213
   Bread of Life 214
   Advocate 215
   The bridegroom 216
   The Author and Finisher of Our Faith 216
   The Chief Cornerstone 217

 King of Kings and Lord of Lords 218
 The Resurrection and the Life 219
 The Word 219
 The Door 220
 The Truth 220
 Saviour 220

Conclusion: Those who know their God will do exploits 223
 Father – Our Father in heaven 225

Altar Call – Call to Salvation 229
 Prayer of Salvation, Author's Version 229

Welcome Letter to new Christians 231
 New Christian To-Do List: 231
 Song: I 'M a New Creation - I 'M a Brand-New Man 232
 Scriptures for Newborn Again Christians 233

Author's Comments 235

About the Author 239

Other Books from the Author 241
 How to Start a Business - A Guide to Starting and Growing a Food Business 241
 Beautiful Foods - The Art of African Catering 241
 Upcoming Books 241
  Wisdom Nuggets from Proverbs 241

Contact Details 243

Works Cited 245
 The Holy Bible 245
 Song: I am a new creation: I am a brand-new man 245

Recommended Resources 247
 The Holy Bible 247

Dedication

I humbly dedicate this book to God the Father, God the Son - Jesus Christ, and God the Holy Spirit, for the divine gift of teaching and wisdom.

ACKNOWLEDGEMENTS

- A massive thank you to my mother, Mrs Rhoda Jolayemi Omolase, who taught me the value of prayer. I learned the virtue and importance of prayer through your morning prayers.
- A big thank you to my prayer mentor, Revd Modupe Babalola, and to every intercessor, who labours daily in the Spirit to bring God's will on earth through consistent prayers.
- Special thanks to my Christian encourager Mrs Toyin Osuntuyi, and Dr Richard Bakare.
- Special thanks to my mastermind partner and husband Tunde Afolalu, my amazing daughter Grace Ife Afolalu, and my wonderful sons Bisi and Pelumi Afolalu.
- I appreciate my family, family in-laws, and every well-wisher in my journey of life especially Mr Tony Egunjobi and Mrs Titi Sylvester.
- Special thanks to my Bible College Provost, Revd Sam O. Adewunmi.
- I thank my friends and my social media (Prayer Nuggets) subscribers, I appreciate you all.
- Best wishes to all my readers, God bless you.

To God be the Glory!

INTRODUCTION

"Those who do wickedly against the covenant he shall corrupt with flattery, but the people who know their God shall be strong and do great exploits."

DANIEL 11:32

The purpose of this book is to gain an understanding of the meaning and the significance of the names of God for use in prayer. An understanding of his names helps Believers (those who believe in God through faith in Jesus Christ) gain insight and wisdom into the attributes and nature of God. God revealed himself to humanity through his names originally in the Hebrew Language which is now available in the English Language.

The names and titles of God explain to us who God is, they are important because, through the names of God, we know who he is, what he likes, and what he dislikes. With the names, we understand the characteristics of God and the benefits of knowing God. Christians who know the names of God, understand him better and enjoy the promises and the goodness of God.

The names help develop the relationship between man and God. The knowledge of God prepares the people of God for a God-fearing and successful life. The Bible states, those who know their

God, will be strong and do great deeds (Daniel 11:32). This scripture means the knowledge of God's name gives Believers courage, confidence, and faith to take outstanding actions like the Acts of the Apostles. With the power in the name of God mixed with boldness, faith and the empowerment of the Holy Spirit, Peter and John healed a crippled man at the gate called Beautiful and they proclaimed the gospel with impressive results of souls and exponential growth for the church (Acts Chapter 3).

The big question is what do we do with the names of God? How do we use the names to relate to God? The Bible gives clear instruction that Christians should bless, praise, magnify, exalt, and worship God with his names. The biblical names of God reveal his power and greatness. The names are meaningful and useful for prayers, particularly prayer of thanksgiving and adoration to God.

We read about biblical characters, who build altars of prayer, worship, and thanksgiving. They gave God new names to celebrate and thank him for the great deeds he helped them to accomplish. A notable example is Abraham, who blessed and named the Lord who supplied him a ram for his sacrifice, Jehovah Jireh (Genesis 22:14). God revealed himself to Moses as the I am that I am (Exodus 3:14). The name helps Believers understand God can be whosoever he chooses to be in their lives. God appears to humankind in various wondrous ways, revealing a part of his nature to them, with his names and deeds.

Believers speak the names of God in praise and prayer, expressing the joy of worshipping him, using his holy names. Below are notable names of God suitable for prayer and worship.

- **The Merciful God** is useful in intercessory prayer. Moses often used the Merciful God to plead with God

to get the Israelites out of God's anger and the threat of destruction.
- **The Prayer of Adoration**, Believers bless God by speaking beautiful words to him, blessing him with his names.
- **The Prayer of Thanksgiving**, Believers use God's names to express their thanks and praise whilst remembering the wonderful works he has done for them.
- **The Prayer of Supplication and Petition,** Believers, call on the names of God in prayer to supply their needs. Jehovah Jireh is used to ask for provision, Jehovah Rapha, for health and healing, the Lord my Shepherd, for provision, comfort, and protection, Jehovah Shalom, for peace and wholeness.

knowing and blessing the names of God is an effective way to honour and seek him in prayer. The knowledge and ability to pray using God's name is the foundation upon which a Believer's relationship with God is built. His unique name Our Father in heaven is the very foundation upon which Christians base their prayers. Christians direct their prayers to God the Father in heaven through the name of his Son Jesus Christ.

> "And whatever you ask in my name, I will do, that the Father may be glorified in the Son."
>
> John 14:13

God's names define the Believer's relationship with him in every aspect of human living, such as provision, protection, and forgiveness of sins through his Son Jesus Christ. Jesus taught his disciples to begin prayer with adoration to the name of God – Our Father. He gave his disciples a prayer model, which is known as the Lord's prayer, when they asked him to teach them how to pray. His model of prayer addresses both human and God's desires. In summary, the model expresses God and human relational needs and sets the terms of the contract of the relationship.

THE LORD'S PRAYER

"Pray like this: Our Father in heaven, may your name be kept holy. May your kingdom come soon. May your will be done on earth, as it is in heaven. Give us today the food we need, and forgive us our sins, as we have forgiven those who sin against us. And don't let us yield to temptation but rescue us from the evil one. If you forgive those who sin against you, your heavenly Father will forgive you. But if you refuse to forgive others, your Father will not forgive your sins."

Matthew 6:9-15

CHAPTER 1

EL SHADDAI - THE ALMIGHTY GOD

"When Abram was ninety-nine years old, the Lord appeared to him and said I am God Almighty, walk before me and be blameless. I will establish my covenant between me and you, and I will multiply you exceedingly."

GENESIS 17:1-2

El Shaddai is translated to the English Language as the Almighty God. The name denotes the mightiness and greatness of God. God appeared to Abraham and brought him out of his homeland asking him to migrate to a new land which he promised to give him and his descendants, a land known as the land flowing with milk and honey (Exodus 13:17). El Shaddai is God's covenant name which he used to define his relationship with Abraham. Abraham found favour with God who chose him as a covenant partner through whom humanity will be saved and blessed.

> "For Abraham will certainly become a great and mighty nation, and all the nations of the earth will be blessed through him."
>
> Genesis 18:18

God followed up on his promise to Abraham, he appeared to Jacob his grandson at Bethel with his name El Shaddai. Jacob the son of Isaac, Abraham's son, had a divine encounter with God El Shaddai, who affirmed his covenant and promise of blessing with his ancestor Abraham. God renewed the promise with Jacob, proving the fact that Abraham's covenant with him will continue through all generations, as he promised Abraham as his reward for obedience, when he tried to sacrifice his son Isaac, as commanded by God (Genesis 22).

> "And through your descendants, all the nations of the earth will be blessed, all because you have obeyed me."
>
> Genesis 22:18

God spoke to Jacob:

> "Then God said, I am El Shaddai, God Almighty. Be fruitful and multiply. You will become a great nation, even many nations and kings will be among your descendants."
>
> Genesis 35:11

The blessing promised by El Shaddai God is associated with prosperity, it symbolises food, provision, and wealth. The promised land of Canaan (now the land of Israel) is a land filled with abundance, a land flowing with milk and honey. God appeared to Moses in the burning bush experience at Horeb, the mountain of God, and confirmed his intention to take the descendants of Abraham, Isaac, and Jacob out of the bondage of slavery in Egypt to their promised land.

> "So, I have come down to rescue them from the power of the Egyptians and lead them out of Egypt into their own fertile and spacious land. It is a land flowing with milk and honey, the land where the Canaanites, Hittites, Amorites, Perizzites, Hivites, and Jebusites now live."
>
> Exodus 3:8

El Shaddai also describes God as the Breast full God. The analogy compares God the Father to a nursing mother because of his ability to support his people and meet their needs as their Jehovah Jireh. The breast full God illustrates God's abundance, which is comparable to the provision given by nursing mothers to their babies. A nursing mother's breast is usually full of milk, thereby, supplying breast milk that has food and nutrients to her baby, the same way God supplies food and drink to his people. Jesus taught Believers to pray to El Shaddai asking for their daily needs (Matthew 6:11). El Shaddai emphasises the aspect and nature of God that supports his people. The name connotes God's benevolence and providence to all of humanity.

> "For you will nurse and be satisfied at her comforting breasts; you will drink deeply and delight in her overflowing abundance."
>
> Isaiah 66:11

> "Give us today our daily bread."
>
> Matthew 6:11

Furthermore, Christians, believe El Shaddai refers to God being a God of sufficiency, Christians often call on the name God of more than enough. This was illustrated in the Bible story of Jacob and Esau. In the story, Jacob cheated his elder brother Esau of their father's firstborn blessing by deceiving him over a bowl of porridge. Jacob fled his homeland to his mother's relative Laban to avoid Esau's wrath and vengeance. On his return, Jacob brought his brother gifts, saying God has blessed him and he had more than enough. Esau resisted taking the gift, also claiming he had enough.

> "But Esau said, I have enough, my brother, keep what you have for yourself."
>
> Genesis 33:9

> "Please take this gift I have brought you, for God has been very gracious to me. I have more than enough. And because Jacob insisted, Esau finally accepted the gift."
>
> Genesis 33:11

El Shaddai also describes the power of God, it suggests a big God who is full of greatness and power with the ability to protect his people. He is a loving Father, who provides, comforts, and protects whoever asks him for help. As a child, my image of God was that of a grandfather with wisdom and power. Someone like Father Christmas with white hair and beard. A giant, but comforting and motherly. A great dad, with an excessively big hand who is ready to save his people. A God who is kind and exceptionally loving.

God Almighty shows human beings the way, He guides and leads his people, offering guidance and divine direction as their shepherd. A notable example is his guidance of Moses and the Israelites in the wilderness on the journey to their promised land (Exodus 13:21).

El Shaddai God appears to his people in divine encounters and transforms their lives. God is a game-changer, whenever he meets his people, he changes their names, transforms their lives, and makes their lives meaningful. Abram became Abraham - the father of nations, Sarai became Sarah - she was transformed from being a barren wife to the fruitful mother of Israel. Jacob the deceiver, became Israel the father of Israel.

PRAYER

El Shaddai, God Almighty, we bless your name and declare you as our provider. We ask that you prosper and bless the work of our hands, in Jesus' name. Amen.

CHAPTER 2

JEHOVAH CHEREB - THE LORD OUR SWORD

"So, Israel will live in safety, Jacob will dwell securely in a land of grain and new wine, where the heavens drop dew. Blessed are you, Israel! Who is like you, a people saved by the LORD? He is your shield and helper and your glorious sword. Your enemies will cower before you, and you will tread on their heights."

DEUTERONOMY 33:28-29

God spoke to the people of Israel and declared himself as their sword. The term sword symbolises power, protection, authority, strength, and courage. A sword is a weapon with a long metal blade and a hilt with a handguard like a cutlass used for cutting or thrusting in battle. It is often used as a symbol of honour and authority. The Lord the Sword, therefore, denotes God as a brave, mighty, and powerful God, with the ability, authority, and power to deliver his people.

God delivers his people from enemies; he protects them from evil. We find examples, of the advantages he gives to his people expressed in his protective relationship with Abraham, and his deliverance of the Israelites, from the Midianites, under the leadership of Gideon. God the Sword fights the Believer's battles and helps them overcome. He is a shield and a protector giving his people the honour of defeating their enemies, spiritually in their affairs of life and physically in battles. So, Christians need not be afraid of their enemies because God is their sword and shield, their defender and protector.

> "After these events, the word of the Lord came to Abram in a vision. Do not be afraid Abram, I am your shield, your very great reward."
>
> Genesis 15:1

> "Then all three groups blew their horns and broke their jars. They held the blazing torches in their left hands and the horns in their right hands, and they all shouted: A sword for the LORD and for Gideon! Each man stood at his position around the camp and watched as all the Midianites rushed around in a panic, shouting as they ran to escape."
>
> Judges 7:20-21

PRAYER

Father, the Lord our Sword, we thank you for your wonderful name. We bless your name and ask that you show up in our lives as our sword, courage, shield, strength, power, protector, and defender, in Jesus' name. Amen.

CHAPTER 3

JEHOVAH SABAOTH - THE LORD OF HOSTS

"Each year Elkanah would travel from his city to worship and to sacrifice to the LORD of hosts at Shiloh, where the two sons of Eli Hophni and Phinehas, were priests of the LORD."

1 SAMUEL 1:3

Jehovah Sabaoth means the Lord of Host. The New Living Bible translation refers to the Lord of Hosts as the Lord of Heaven's armies. Jehovah Sabaoth denotes God as the Lord of the Israelites' armies. The name is reassuring because it declares God is the defender and deliverer of his people. As the Lord of Hosts, God is all-powerful, which means he has authority, and power. He is the redeemer, protector, and captain of warfare, winning every battle for his people, giving them justice and victory as their Lord of Hosts.

> "Our Redeemer, the Lord of Host is his name. He is the Holy One of Israel"

> Isaiah 47:4

The Lord of Hosts implies God is the leader of all armies, both heaven, and earth. The Bible states, God will lead both armies of angels and human beings, to defeat Satan and his demons in the future (Revelations (19:11-20). Whatever warfare, or attack, the children of God suffer, they can confidently depend on and call on the name of God, the Lord of Hosts. The Bible tells the story of how God supplied an army of angels, leading horses, and chariots of fire to protect prophet Elisha (2 Kings 6:17-20).

> "Elisha prayed: O Lord, open his eyes so he may see. Then the Lord opened the servant's eyes and he looked and saw the hills full of horses and chariots of fire all around Elisha."

> 2 Kings 6:17

God protects his people with the hosts of heaven's angels and armies. God commands his angels to guard, shield, and protect every Believer in Christ Jesus.

> "He will order his angels to protect you, wherever you may go"

> Psalm 91:11

PRAYER

It is my prayer, that the Lord of Host, will become real to you personally. I pray, that your eyes of understanding, will open to see the great armies of angels around you, in Jesus' name. Amen.

CHAPTER 4

EL HANNUM - THE GRACIOUS GOD

"And the Lord passed before him and proclaimed. The Lord, the Lord God, merciful, and gracious, longsuffering, and abundant in goodness, and truth"

EXODUS 34:6

Gracious means someone kind, pleasant, good, and courteous towards people, particularly those of lower status. The name describes the goodness and grace of God. He is a Gracious God, whose graciousness extends to the whole of humanity. His providence is available to everyone even those who do not deserve his goodness. The Gracious God captures the grace of God, which is the very essence of his divinity, the name portrays his merciful nature and kindness. God is compassionate, forgiving, lenient, and good. Jehovah El Hannum is good to all, his compassion rests on all his creation.

> "They will extol the fame of your abundant goodness and sing joyfully of your righteousness. The Lord is gracious and compassionate, slow to anger, and abounding in loving devotion. The Lord is good to all, and his compassion rests on all he has made."
>
> Psalm 145:7-9

God is good and his goodness, love, and mercy, endures forever, throughout all generations.

> "For the Lord is good, and his love endures forever, his faithfulness continues through all generations."
>
> Psalm 100:5

Prophets, psalmists, leaders in the Bible, and Jesus Christ testified to the goodness and graciousness of God.

> "The Lord is good, a stronghold in the day of trouble, and he knows those who take refuge in him."
>
> Nahum 1:7

> "For you Lord, are good, and ready to forgive, and abundant in loving kindness to all who call upon you."
>
> Psalm 86:5

> "And Jesus said to him, why do you call me good? No one is good except God alone."
>
> Mark 10:18

It is worth noting that the gracious nature of God does not always generate a positive reaction from people. Whilst Moses appreciated and worshipped the Gracious God (Exodus 34:6), Jonah protested in anger of the graciousness and mercy of God when God forgave the people of Nineveh of their sin and relented in his threat to completely wipe them out (Jonah 4:2). God is slow to anger, he is compassionate and abounding in love, he relents from sending calamity on humanity. Believers, therefore, are called to the act of thanksgiving, praising his name, the Gracious God. The Bible says to give thanks to the Lord, for he is good, his mercy endures forever. (Psalm 136:1 and 1 Chronicles 16:34).

PRAYER

Let us thank the Lord, our Gracious God, let us bow down and worship his holy name. We pray his abundant mercy, love, and graciousness, will rest upon every Believer forever and ever in Jesus' name. Amen.

CHAPTER 5

EL ELYON - THE MOST-HIGH GOD

*"I cry out to God most high, to God
who fulfills his purpose for me."*

PSALM 57:2

Jehovah El Elyon means the Most-High God. The name describes the greatness of God as the highest God in the universe. God has all authority in heaven and on earth. The term High announces God's superiority and sovereignty over all creation, he is Almighty God. There is no other god before him, neither is there anything in heaven, on earth, nor under the earth that should be worshipped or exalted above God.

The Most-High God is highly exalted, he delivers his people from their enemies and oppressors. Moses and his sister Miriam celebrated the delivery of the Israelites from their Egyptian oppressors with a song of praise exalting the highest God.

> "I will sing to the Lord, for he is highly exalted. Both horse and driver he has hurled into the sea."
>
> Exodus 15:1

The Book of Psalms declares no one can fathom the greatness of God, because he is the Highest God with the awesome ability to perform glorious deeds which no other gods can do. He is, therefore, the King of Kings and the Lord of Lords, the blessed and only ruler of the universe who is greatly to be praised in heaven and on earth.

> "For, at just the right time, Christ will be revealed from heaven by the blessed and only almighty God, the King of Kings and Lord of Lords. He alone can never die, and he lives in light so brilliant that no human can approach him. No human eye has ever seen him, nor ever will. All honour and power to him forever! Amen."
>
> 1 Timothy 6:15-16

Christians are confident that the Highest God will perform and perfect all that concerns them. Apostle Paul declares that God begins and completes his excellent work in the lives of his people.

> "Being confident of this, that he who began a decent work in you will carry it on to completion until the day of Christ Jesus."
>
> Philippians 1:6

PRAYER

Let us pray, that the Lord Most High God, will perfect all that concerns us in Jesus' name. Amen.

Chapter 6

Elohim Bashamayim - The God in Heaven

"Acknowledge and take to heart this day, that the Lord is God in Heaven above and on the earth below. There is no other."

Deuteronomy 4:39

Jehovah Elohim Bashamayin informs us of the location of God. The name is a revelation of God's home and work address. Heaven is the throne of God, his reigning centre, and from there, he rules the nations, the universe, and reigns in the affairs of mankind. We can assume that his workplace and head office is heaven which is his throne room. Isaiah saw the Lord seated on his throne room in heaven. He gave a description of his holiness and the beauty of God's glory filling the throne room (Isaiah 6). God the Son also lives in heaven according to the accounts in the Gospels.

> "When the Lord Jesus had finished talking with them, he was taken up into heaven and sat down in the place of honour at God's right hand."
>
> Mark 16:19

We know from scripture, that Jesus is working in heaven praying for his people, so heaven is God's throne.

> "Who then will condemn us? No one, for Christ Jesus died for us and was raised to life for us, and he is sitting in the place of honour at God's right hand, interceding for us."
>
> Romans 8:34

God lives in heaven, and from there, he hears our prayers. The prayer of King Jehoshaphat confirms that we pray to God of the Heavens, and he answers our prayers.

The Prayer of King Jehoshaphat

> "Jehoshaphat stood in the assembly of Judah, and Jerusalem in the house of the Lord, before the new court and said: "O Lord the God of our fathers, are you not God in the heavens? And are you not ruler over all the kingdoms of the nations? Power and might are in your hands, so that no one, can stand against you."
>
> 2 Chronicles 20:6

God also fills the whole earth; the Bible says the earth is his footstool.

> "This is what the Lord says: Heaven is my throne, and the earth is my footstool. Where is the house you will build for me? Where is my resting place?"
>
> Isaiah 66:1

Believers cannot use the names of God in vain, neither can they swear by his dwelling place.

> "But I tell you not to swear at all: either by heaven, for it is God's throne; or by the earth, for it is his footstool, or by Jerusalem, for it is the city of the great King."
>
> Matthew 5:34-35

We serve the God of Heavens, the creator of heaven, earth, and all creation. He is a great and formidable God, who alone rides the heavens.

> "Yours, Lord, is the greatness, the power, and the glory. The victory and the majesty, for all that is in heaven and the earth, is yours. Yours is the kingdom; O Lord and you are exalted as head overall."
>
> 1 Chronicle 29:11

PRAYER

O Lord God in heaven, we exalt your name above all other names. We seek your face, show us your love, power, and might. To you alone be the power and the glory, in Jesus' name. Amen.

Chapter 7

Elohim Kedoshim - The Holy God

"There is no one holy like the LORD, there is no one besides you, there is no Rock like our God."

1 SAMUEL 2:2

Holy means sacred, a state of being good, blameless, and morally upstanding. The Holy God means a God who is good, pure and without sin or blemish. This definition truly captures who God is as a glorious God. Isaiah amazed by his holiness, glory, perfection, and the beauty of his presence cried out: "Woe to me, I am ruined! For I am a man of unclean lips" (Isaiah 6:5). The glory and holiness of God were like a mirror for him to see his human filthiness and sin. He described the worship of God's holiness in heaven by the angels who were calling to one another:

> Holy, holy, holy is the Lord Almighty, the whole earth is full of his glory."
>
> Isaiah 6:3

The Book of Revelation also described the holiness of God filling the throne room in heaven. It gives a similar account to Isaiah's vision of God's holiness, glory, and worship in heaven by the angels and the elders.

> "Each of the four living creatures had six wings and was covered under its wings. Day and night they never stop saying: Holy, holy, holy is the Lord God Almighty, who was, and is, and is to come.
>
> Whenever the living beings give glory and honour and thanks to the one sitting on the throne (the one who lives forever and ever), the twenty-four elders fall before him who sit on the throne and worship him who lives forever and ever.
>
> They lay their crowns before the throne and say: You are worthy, our Lord and God, to receive glory, honour, and power, for you created all things, and by your will, they were created and have their being."
>
> Revelation 4:8-11

God is a holy God; the beauty of his holiness is expressed in the scriptures. And his holiness is worthy of worship, Jesus said to hallow his name because he is Holy (Matthew 6). And the Psalmist says to exalt the Holy God.

> "Exalt the Lord our God, and worship, at his Holy hill, for the Lord our God is Holy."
>
> Psalm 99:9

The scriptures ascribe holiness to God because he is holy. God expects and demands holiness from his people. He asked Abraham to be faithful and blameless which means to live a holy life (Genesis 17:1). The Character of God the Son is perfect, so Believers should follow in his example to help them live a holy life as Christians and children of God Almighty because God desires his people to live outstanding and upright lives.

> "Because it is written, you shall be Holy, for I am Holy."
>
> 1 Peter 1:16

The Holy God is worthy of praise because, in him, holiness is imputed to Christians. Therefore, in appreciation of the holiness of God, Christians should praise and rejoice in Jehovah Elohim Kedoshim - the Holy God.

> "Who is like You among the gods, O Lord? Who is like You, majestic in holiness, impressive in praises, working wonders?"
>
> Exodus 15:11

> "Then, I will praise you with music on the harp because you are faithful to your promises, O my

God. I will sing praises to you with a lyre, O Holy One of Israel."

Psalm 71:22

> **PRAYER**
> *Father Lord, Elohim Kedoshim, we pray for holiness and sanctification by your word and spirit in Jesus' name. Amen.*

Chapter 8

El Emeth - The God of Truth

"Into your hand, I commit my spirit. You have redeemed me, O Lord God of truth."

PSALM 31:5

The God of Truth is a unique name because it denotes the integrity and truthful nature of God. Truth means the quality of being true, it implies God is trustworthy and honest. The Bible declares, God cannot lie because he has a pure and honest character. Whatever he says or promise to do for his people, he will perform. This means God keeps his promises, he is a promise keeper who fulfills his word.

"As the rain and the snow come down from heaven, and do not return to it without watering the earth and making it bud and flourish, so that it yields seed for the Sower and bread for the eater, so, is my word that goes out from my mouth. It will not return to me empty but will accomplish what I desire and achieve the purpose for which I sent it."

Isaiah 55:10 -11

"For no matter how many promises God has made, they are "Yes" in Christ. And so, through him, the Amen is spoken by us to the glory of God."

2 Corinthians 1:20

"God is not human, that he should lie, not a human being that he should change his mind. Does he speak and then not act? Does he promise and not fulfill?"

Numbers 23:19

"So, God has given both his promise and his oath. These two things are unchangeable because it is impossible for God to lie. Therefore, we who have fled to him for refuge can have great confidence as we hold to the hope that lies before us."

Hebrews 6:18

The Bible portrays God as sincere and faithful to his word, a God of truth who is dependable and reliable. This is clear in the words of his Son Jesus Christ at his death, the Bible records he surrendered his spirit to God's safekeeping.

> "Then, Jesus called out in a loud voice: Father into your hands, I commit my spirit. And when he has said this, he breathed his last."
>
> Luke 23:46

Jesus' action of surrender proves the fact that God is dependable and trustworthy. Stephen similarly committed his spirit into God's hands (Acts 7:59). These being the last words of these great men, is evidence of God's trustworthiness. Believers can rightly conclude that God is a God of Truth. My opinion is that no one will commit their precious soul to God if he is a God that fails his people.

> "Not one word of all the Lord's good promises to Israel failed, everyone was fulfilled."
>
> Joshua 21:45

> "For no word from God will ever fail."
>
> Luke 1:37

Apostle Paul wrote to Timothy his disciple, testifying to the loyalty and faithfulness of the God of Truth.

> "That is why I am suffering as I am. Yet, this is no cause for shame because I know whom I have believed. And I am convinced that he can guard what I have entrusted to him until that day."
>
> 2 Timothy 1:12

PRAYER

Father, God of Truth, we thank you for your truthful nature. You are a promise keeper, we trust you God of Truth. We pray that you sanctify every Believer with your word and keep Christians on the path of truth and righteousness in Jesus' name. Amen.

Chapter 9

Elohim Yeshuati - God of Our Salvation

> *"The Lord is my strength and my song, and he has become my salvation; he is my God, and I will praise him, my father's God, and I will exalt him."*
>
> EXODUS 15:2

Elohim Yeshuati means the God of my Salvation. The term salvation means preservation or deliverance from harm, loss, or ruin. At the beginning of the world, the first man Adam committed the sin of disobedience which gave the devil the upper hand over humankind. This account is mentioned in the Book of Genesis Chapter 3. God stepped in to save humanity from the damnation of spiritual death which was the consequence of sin. He gave up his only begotten son to die to atone for sin. Biblical salvation is, therefore, deliverance from sin and its consequences, which Christians believe is obtained by faith in Christ.

The name Elohim Yeshuati explains the work of redemption. God gave humanity, the gift of eternal life through the death of his only son Jesus Christ. Christians are redeemed by the precious blood of Jesus Christ. We are the Redeemed of the Lord because Jesus Christ, paid the wages of sin, which is death. He died on the cross of Calvary, shedding his blood to atone for the sin of human beings.

Therefore, the God of Salvation, should be praised and adored, because in him we have freedom from sin, and we have been given, everything that pertains to life and godliness to live a godly life in Christ Jesus our God of Salvation.

> "His divine power has given us everything we need for a godly life through our knowledge of him who called us by his glory and goodness."
>
> 2 Peter 1:3

> "The Lord is my strength and my shield; my heart trusts in him, and he helps me. My heart leaps for joy, and with my song, I praise him. The Lord is the strength of his people, a fortress of salvation for the anointed one."
>
> Psalm 28:7-8

Salvation is available to everyone who calls upon the name of the Lord. The Bible says those who believe Jesus is the Messiah (the anointed Christ) and confess with their mouth that Jesus is Lord will be saved (obtain salvation).

"For God so loved the world, that he gave his only begotten son, that whosoever believes in him should not perish, but have everlasting life."

John 3:16

PRAYER

O Lord God of Salvation, we praise you, we thank you, for the work of redemption, through the sacrifice of the Lord Jesus Christ. We ask that you save those who call on your name in Jesus' name. Amen.

CHAPTER 10

EL GIBBOR - THE MIGHTY GOD

"You show love to thousands but bring the punishment for the parents' sins into the laps of their children after them. Great and mighty God, whose name is the LORD Almighty."

JEREMIAH 32:18

Mighty symbolises power and strength, so, the name Mighty God connotes the power and strength of God. He is the Omnipotent God with unlimited power. The Mighty God is like Almighty God or El Shaddai which denotes the strength, benevolence, and awesomeness of God. The name describes God's nature and attributes as strong, mighty, and powerful. Believers, understand God's courage, bravery, warfare, and power through this name. The Mighty God became manifest to humanity in his Son Jesus Christ. Prophet Isaiah prophesied about Jesus coming as the Mighty God.

> "For unto us a child is born, unto us a son is given, and the government will be upon his shoulders. And he will be called Wonderful Counsellor, Mighty God, Everlasting Father, Prince of Peace."
>
> Isaiah 9:6

The scripture explains God is not just mighty in physical strength, he is mighty in counsel, wisdom, and understanding.

> "You are great in counsel and mighty in deeds, for your eyes are open to the ways of the sons of men, to give everyone according to his ways and according to the fruit of his doings."
>
> Jeremiah 32:19

Prophet Jeremiah illustrated the mightiness of God in his prayer after he bought a field, during the impending captivity of the Israelites by the Babylonians.

The Prayer of Jeremiah

> "After I had given the deed of purchase to Baruch son of Neriah, I prayed to the Lord: Ah, Sovereign LORD, you have made the heavens and the earth by your great power and outstretched arm.

Nothing is too hard for you. You show love to thousands but bring the punishment for parents' sins into the laps of their children after them.

Great and mighty God, whose name is the LORD Almighty. Great are your purposes and mighty are your deeds. Your eyes are open to the ways of all mankind, you reward each person according to their conduct and as their deeds deserve.

You performed signs and wonders in Egypt and have continued them to this day, in Israel and among all mankind, and have gained the renown that is still yours.

You brought your people Israel out of Egypt with signs and wonders, by a mighty hand and an outstretched arm and with great terror.

You gave them this land, you had sworn to give their ancestors, a land flowing with milk and honey."

Jeremiah 32:16-22

Jeremiah emphasised in his prayer that nothing is too difficult for the mighty God. God confirmed this in his response to Jeremiah's prayer.

GOD'S RESPONSE TO JEREMIAH'S PRAYER

> "Then the word of the LORD came to Jeremiah. I am the LORD, the God of all mankind. Is there anything too hard for me?"
>
> Jeremiah 32:27

An awareness that Believers serve a mighty God, helps them to conduct and take great actions (signs and wonders). Christians have confidence and trust in God's name and his ability to empower them to excel in every aspect of life. It is a joy to know that Christians serve a mighty God whose power knows no limit. The Book of the Acts of the Apostles is a demonstration of the power of God made clear in the works and deeds of the Apostles. They ascribed their success to their faith in the mighty power of the name of Jesus, coupled with their boldness, courage, and the empowerment of the Holy Spirit.

Believers will, therefore, do great and mighty deeds in the name of Jesus Christ, the Mighty God, if they believe in the power of his name.

PRAYER

Father, the Mighty God, we thank you for your mighty power, we pray you to do great and mighty deeds, through whoever believes in you, to the glory of your name, in Jesus' name. Amen.

Chapter 11

El Gemuah - The God of Recompense

"Then I will compensate you for the years that the swarming locust has eaten, the creeping locust, the stripping locust, and the gnawing locust, my great army which I sent among you."

JOEL 2:25

Recompense means to compensate or make amends to someone for a loss or harm suffered. God is a God of Recompense which means God makes amends to his people when they suffer a loss or harm. Insurance companies sell protection policies to indemnify and protect people against losses. The insurer offers monetary compensation, in times of loss to protect the insured person or their loved ones against financial hardship. God divinely supports his people as their God of Recompense compensating their loss.

The God of Recompense offers his people, protection from the hardships of losses spiritually, emotionally, financially, and physically. God supernaturally rectifies unfair losses. In addition, he offers retribution whenever necessary because he is the God who avenges his people. Christians ought to rejoice in his name the God of Recompense because, in addition to compensating his people, he saves them and replace their shame with his glory and joy.

> "Say to those with anxious heart, take courage, fear not. Behold, your God will come with vengeance. The recompense of God will come. He will save you."
>
> Isaiah 35:4

> "You shall eat in plenty and be satisfied, and praise the name of the Lord your God, who has dealt wondrously with you, and my people will never be put to shame."
>
> Joel 2:26

PRAYER

Dear Lord, the God of Recompense, we bless and honour your name. We ask that you grant us compensation in every area of life. Reward the works of our labour and grant us rest in Jesus' name. Amen.

CHAPTER 12

JEHOVAH BORE - THE LORD THE CREATOR

"Do you not know, have you not heard? The Lord is the everlasting God, the creator of the ends of the earth. He will not grow tired or weary."

ISAIAH 40:28

Jehovah Bore confirms that God is the creator of heaven and earth. The Book of Genesis explains to humanity, how everything began. Though there are theories disputing the existence of God, and the fact that God created human beings and everything else, Christians believe in the creation account record in the Bible.

The account that God created the heavens, and the earth is more plausible than the scientific theories that are not yet proven. We know from scriptures, that God created all things through his divine wisdom and understanding.

"In the beginning, God created the heavens and the earth."

Genesis 1:1

"Being through God, and apart from Him, nothing came into being, that has come into being."

John 1:3

"The Lord by wisdom founded the earth. And by understanding, he established the heavens."

Proverb 3:19

PRAYER

Dear Lord, we bless your holy name - Jehovah Bore. We give you thanks for creating all things, they are good, so, we praise you, the Lord our Creator, in Jesus' name. Amen.

CHAPTER 13

ELOHIM CHAYIM - THE LIVING GOD

"David said: Who is this uncircumcised Philistine, that he should defy the armies of the Living God?"

1 SAMUEL 17:26

Elohim Chayim, the Living God, means God is alive. A living thing is a person, animal, or plant that is not dead. They are usually alert and active. The revelation that God is living emphasises the fact that our God is alive. This knowledge empowers the people of God to do great exploits. A notable example is the impressive deeds of David in the Bible story of David and Goliath. David, armed with the knowledge, that the God of Israel is the living God who has power and might, killed Goliath, a Philistine soldier described as a giant. David conquered an entire army, even though he was a youth with no military experience (1 Samuel 17).

The revelation given by the name Elohim Chayim, helps believers understand the omnipotent, omnipresent, and omniscient God, who is alive, can save, and deliver his people. Christians believe in the existence of a living God. The Bible says the God of Heavens is not dead, he is alive. Christians declare during the Easter celebration of the resurrection of Christ Jesus, that Jesus is alive! He is alive because he died and rose again by the resurrection power of God. Because of this fact, Believers in Christ Jesus believe they will have eternal life (life after death).

> "Jesus said to her, I am the resurrection and the life. The one who believes in me will live, even though they die."
>
> John 11:25

Elijah made a mockery of idol worshippers who serve dead gods. He challenged Baal worshippers to get Baal their god, to consume their sacrifice by fire. The god of Baal did not show up because it is a non-living fabricated idol. A dead god that is mute, blind, with no power to save or deliver his worshippers.

> "And they took the bull that was given to them, prepared it, and called on the name of Baal from morning until noon shouting "O Baal answer us!" But there was no sound and no one answered. As they leapt around the altar they had made, at noon, Elijah began to taunt them, saying "Shout louder for he is god! Perhaps, he is deep in thought or occupied, or on a journey. Perhaps he is sleeping and must be awakened." So, they shouted louder and

cut themselves with knives and lances as was their custom until the blood gushed over them."

1 Kings 18:26-28

What a sight! The test proves that God is alive, and confirms the fact, that idols are dead. They can neither see, hear, nor speak, the Living God, on the other hand, is alive and well. He consumed Elijah's sacrifice with fire because he is a consuming fire (1 Kings 18:38).

THE PRAYER OF ELIJAH

"At the time of sacrifice, the prophet Elijah stepped forward and prayed: LORD, the God of Abraham, Isaac, and Israel, let it be known today that you are God in Israel and that I am your servant and have done all these things at your command. Answer me, LORD, answer me, so these people will know that you, LORD, are God, and that you are turning their hearts back again.

Then the fire of the Lord fell and burned up the sacrifice, the wood, the stones, and the soil, and licked up the water in the trench. When all the people saw this, they fell face down on the ground and cried: The LORD - he is God! The LORD – he is God!"

1 Kings 18:36-39

PRAYER

Lord our Living God, we praise your living name. We ask, that you answer our prayers whenever we call on you in Jesus' name. Amen.

CHAPTER 14

JEHOVAH MAGINNENU - THE LORD OUR DEFENCE

"The Lord is our defence, and the Holy One of Israel is our King."

PSALM 89:18

The Hebrew name of God, Jehovah Maginnenu translates as God our Defence in the English Language. Defence means the action of defending or resisting attack, so the name informs the people of God that God is a defender and a protector. He is the Believer's shield, buckler, and helper. This name is particularly useful for prayers against spiritual wickedness and attacks from the devil.

Apostle Paul taught the Ephesians about spiritual warfare. He gave them warfare strategies, advising them to remain strong but calm whilst resisting the devil during spiritual warfare, doing their part spiritually, physically, prayerfully, and leaving the rest to God who saves the upright in heart (Ephesians 6:10-18).

Apostle Paul's Spiritual Warfare Strategies

"Finally, be strong in the Lord and his mighty power. Put on the full armour of God, so that you can take your stand against the devil's schemes. For our struggle is not against flesh and blood, but against the rulers, against the authorities, against the powers of this dark world and against the spiritual forces of evil in the heavenly realms.

Therefore, put on the full armour of God, so that when the day of evil comes, you may be able to stand your ground, and after you have done everything, to stand.

Stand firm then, with the belt of truth buckled around your waist, with the breastplate of righteousness in place, and with your feet fitted with the readiness that comes from the gospel of peace, in addition to all this, take up the shield of faith, with which you can extinguish all the flaming arrows of the evil one.

Take the helmet of salvation the sword of the Spirit, which is the word of God. And pray in the Spirit on all occasions with all kinds of prayers and requests.

Be alert and always keep on praying for all the Lord's people."

Ephesians 6:10-18

The revelation that God is our defence, should give the people of God courage. Christians ought not to fear the devil, because they serve a God who defends his people and those who live in the shelter of the Most-High will be safe (Psalm 91:1). God our Defence is the Believer's shield and refuge. He is our high tower, strength, and stronghold. God encouraged Joshua to be courageous and fear not because he is with him.

> "This is my command; be strong and courageous! Do not be afraid or discouraged. For the Lord, your God is with you, wherever you go."

Joshua 1:9

The Lord our Defence is an encourager. He empowers his people with courage and strength. He is ever-present to fight their battles and deliver them from the evil one. Therefore, Christians should take courage in God, and fear no evil.

A Psalm of David

> "The Lord is my light and my salvation, whom shall, I fear? The Lord is the strength of my life, of whom shall I be afraid? When the wicked came against me to eat up my flesh, my enemies, and foes, they stumbled and fell.

Though an army may encamp against me, my heart shall not fear. Though war may rise against me, in this I will be confident.

One thing I have desired of the Lord, that will I seek: That I may dwell in the house of the Lord all the days of my life, to behold the beauty of the Lord, and to inquire in his temple."

Psalm 27:1-4

PRAYER

O Lord, God our Defence, we rejoice in your name daily, we ask that you show yourself strong in our lives. Be our defender, and our helper, in times of trouble, in Jesus' name. Amen.

CHAPTER 15

EL HAKKABOD - THE GOD OF GLORY

"The Lord is upon the waters, the God of Glory thunders. The Lord thunders over the mighty waters. The voice of the Lord is powerful. The voice of the Lord is majestic."

PSALM 29:3-4

El Hakkabod means the God of Glory, the word means magnificence, greatness, holiness, beauty, or honour. Glory depicts not just the beauty and splendour of the spirit of God, but also the beauty of his character, and nature. The Bible describes glory as being the light of God. The light, penetrates darkness, forcing it away from the people of God. The God of Glory shines his light over his people, he makes them radiate glory, beauty, goodness, and splendour. God described his glory as his goodness and compassion when Moses asked him to show him his glory.

> "Then Moses said, now show me your glory."
>
> Exodus 33:18

> "The Lord replied, I will make my goodness pass before you, and I will call out my name, Yahweh, before you. For I will show mercy to anyone I choose, and I will show compassion to anyone I choose."
>
> Exodus 33:19

The glory of God radiates from his face, when God shines his face upon his people, they receive his blessing, radiance, anointing and goodness. The Bible likens this experience to God smiling on his people.

> "May the Lord smile on you and be gracious to you."
>
> Numbers 6:25 (New Living Bible Translation)

> "Arise, shine, for your light has come, and the glory of the Lord rises upon you. See, darkness covers the earth, and thick darkness is over the people, but the Lord rises upon you and his glory appears over you."
>
> Isaiah 60:1-2

God's glory fills the earth and the beauty of all his creation speaks of his glory. We only need to look around us to see the beauty and glory of God in his creation. The birds singing, the animals, the oceans, the plants and flowers, human beings of various nations and beauty, the rainbow, the sun, the moon, and the firmaments of the sky. The glory of God fills the heavens, Isaiah saw his

Glory, and described the worship of angels in heaven celebrating God's glory (Isaiah 6).

> "They were calling out to each other: Holy, holy, holy, is the Lord of Heaven's Armies! The whole earth is filled with his glory!"
>
> Isaiah 6:3

The glory of God sometimes appears like a cloud which Christians believe to be the physical glory of the anointing of God. The Bible records God's glory appearing to his people like a thick cloud to either protect or lead them, as in the time of the Israelites' journey through the wilderness.

> "And the Lord went before them by day in a pillar of cloud to lead the way, and by night in a pillar of fire to give them light, to go by day and night."
>
> Exodus 13:21

> "Then the Lord will create over all of Mount Zion, and over those who assemble there, a cloud of smoke by day and a glow of flaming fire by night over everything, the glory will be a canopy."
>
> Isaiah 4:5

PRAYER

Father king of Glory, let your glorious name be praised, forever; and let the whole earth be filled with your glory in Jesus' name. Amen.

Chapter 16

Jehovah Jireh - The Lord Shall Provide

> *"And Abraham called the name of that place Jehovah Jireh as it is said to this day, in the mount of the Lord, it shall be seen."*
>
> **Genesis 22:14**

Jehovah Jireh is a special name about the ability of God to support his people and provide for their needs. The name was mentioned in the Book of Genesis 22. God asked Abraham to sacrifice his son Isaac to him. However, God showed up at the place of the sacrifice with a ram for the sacrifice in place of Isaac. Therefore, Abraham did not have to kill his son. He was thankful, so he worshipped God with the name Jehovah Jireh meaning the Lord shall provide. The name means God will support his people financially as their source of provision.

It is believed that the test to sacrifice Isaac to God is a sign of God's willingness to sacrifice his son Jesus Christ as the sacrificial lamb that will take away the sin of the world. It is worth noting that Abraham's passing the test, reassured God the Father that human beings can be saved. The disobedience of the first man Adam caused the downfall of man, and the obedience of the last man Jesus restored man to God. The obedience and faith of Abraham began the restoration process of the relationship between man and God. Abraham received the gift of the blessing of God and became the father of faith with the promise that his seed will own the gate of his enemies.

Jehovah Jireh has since become a popular name of God amidst Christians. Believers pray for God's provision and thank him for his providence using the name of God - The Lord who provides. Paul the Apostle sent a letter from prison to the Philippians recommending that they ought not to be anxious for their daily needs, but to make supplications to God who provides.

> "And my God will supply every need of yours according to his riches in glory in Christ Jesus."
>
> Philippians 4:19

Jesus also taught his disciples to ask God for their daily needs in the Lord's prayer (Matthew 6).

> "Give us today our daily bread."
>
> Matthew 6:11

PRAYER

The Lord our Provider, we thank you that you are our source financially. We bless your marvellous name - Jehovah Jireh. We ask that you supply us with our daily needs. Give us our daily bread O Lord – our Jehovah Jireh in Jesus' name, we pray. Amen.

CHAPTER 17

EL ROI - THE GOD WHO SEES

"She gave this name to the Lord who spoke to her: You are the God who sees me, for she said I have now seen the One who sees me."

GENESIS 16:13

El Roi means the Lord who sees me. This is a name, which proves the fact, that God is not a respecter of persons. The name was given to God, by Hagar, an Egyptian servant. She was Sarah's maidservant, whom she bestowed on Abraham as a concubine when Sarah could not bear him a son. However, when Hagar became pregnant, she began to despise Sarah. Thereby, arousing her anger, Sarah mistreated her, causing her to flee from the household of Abraham.

On her journey in the desert when running away, an angel of the Lord appeared to her near a spring of water. The angel informed her of the birth of her son Ishmael and instructed her to go back and submit herself to her head of household. She praised and worshipped the God who can see in a time of need, giving him, the name the Lord who sees me, El Roi. Jehovah El Roi is the name of God, who brings Believers fresh hope. It is a reminder, that God sees and helps his people in times of need, discouragement, loneliness, and despair. Christians should learn from this name of God, not to be fearful or anxious because God sees.

Hagar had another experience in the wilderness when she and her son Ishmael were evicted, to prevent Ishmael from sharing in the inheritance with Isaac, Sarah's son. She left the household of Abraham with her son; her water ran out in the journey in the desert. She began to sob, afraid, her son Ishmael will die. An angel of God called to her from heaven and opened her eyes to see a well of water which she gave to her son to drink (Genesis 21:8-21).

Hagar's two experiences with the Lord teach Believers to trust in God, to never be anxious or fret over life circumstances. Jesus and Apostle Paul emphasised this lesson in their teachings.

> "Therefore, I tell you, do not be anxious about your life, what you will eat or what you will drink nor about your body, what you will wear. Is not life more than food and the body more than clothing? Look at the birds of the air they neither sow nor reap nor gather into barns and yet your heavenly Father feeds them. Are you not of more value than they? And which of you being anxious can add a single hour to his span of life?"
>
> Matthew 6:25-27

"Do not be anxious about anything, but in every situation, by prayer and petition, with thanksgiving, present your request to God."

Philippians 4:6

In the first experience, God showed up in Hagar's life to give her counsel, guidance, and direction of life in her confused state of mind. And in the second experience, she received provision. Therefore, Christians are encouraged to take their requests, and worries to God in prayer, and supplication. The Lord who sees will resolve every issue of life with his infinite wisdom and counsel because he is the Omniscient God, the Lord who knows everything and sees all things - The Lord who sees!

PRAYER

The Lord God who sees, we bless your holy name. We ask that you see us and meet us at our points of need, in Jesus' name. Amen. "May God grant your heart desires and make all your plans succeed." Psalm 20: 4

Chapter 18

El Emunah - The Faithful God

> *"Moses said, because the Lord loved you, and kept the oath he swore to your fathers. He brought you out with a mighty hand, and redeemed you from the house of slavery, from the hand of Pharoah king of Egypt. Know, therefore, that the Lord your God is God, the faithful God, who keeps his covenant of loving devotion, for a thousand generations of those who love him, and keep his commandments."*
>
> DEUTERONOMY 7:8-9

The name of God, El Emunah expresses the faithfulness of God. The word faithful means to be loyal, constant, or steadfast. This name of God explains the loyalty and unyielding nature of God. He keeps his promises and his word. God made a covenant between him and Abraham, promising him blessings for several generations (Genesis 17:7). God brought the people of Israel out of the captivity of slavery. He established them in the promised land, a land flowing with milk and honey per his promise to their ancestor, Abraham.

The faithfulness of God is one great characteristic of the Living God. He is faithful and keeps his word to his people. He performs his promises and remains faithful, even when his people are faithless.

> "God who has called you into fellowship with His son Jesus Christ our Lord is faithful."
>
> 1 Corinthians 1:9

> "The one who calls you is faithful, and he will do it."
>
> 1 Thessalonians 5:24

> "If we are faithless, he remains faithful, for he cannot deny himself."
>
> 2 Timothy 2:13

God is firm, a solid rock, who stays constant, and is forever the same. Whatever he promises to do for his people, he will act and fulfil it (Numbers 23:19) Hallelujah!

PRAYER

El Emunah, our Faithful Father, we give you thanks for your faithfulness throughout all generations. We ask you to walk with us, as our Faithful Father, even when our faith waivers in Jesus' name. Amen.

Chapter 19

Jehovah Ori - The Lord Our Light

"The Lord is my light and salvation, so why should I be afraid? The Lord is my fortress, protecting me from danger, so why should I tremble?"

PSALM 27:1

Light is a source of illumination, which makes people see in darkness. God created the light to illuminate the darkness of the world during creation. The Bible states, in the beginning, God commanded the darkness to break forth into light (Genesis 1:3). Apart from the physical light of the sun, the moon, and the stars, God himself is light. He is the spiritual light that illuminates the world and penetrates through spiritual darkness.

> "The city does not need the sun or the moon to shine on it, for the glory of God gives it light, and the Lamb is its lamp."
>
> Revelation 21:23

The sin of disobedience of the first man Adam brought the curse of darkness on humanity. So, God gave up his only begotten son, to bring light and redemption, to whoever put their faith in Jesus Christ his Son. Prophet Isaiah spoke of the coming of the Lord that will bring light to the world. Jesus fulfilled what was said through the prophet Isaiah in the Gospel (Matthew 4:16).

> "The people walking in darkness have seen a great light, on those living in the land of the shadows of death a light has dawned."
>
> Isaiah 9:2, Matthew 4:16

The Bible declares God is light (1 John 1:5), his light illuminates, guides, and directs the path of those who put their trust in him. God our Light gives his people light to overcome darkness especially the shadows of death. There are testimonies of people who see a tunnel of light at the point of death.

> "Even though I walk through the valley of the shadow of death, I will fear no evil, for you are with me, your rod and staff, they comfort me."
>
> Psalm 23:4

God our light, guides Believers through this world, with spiritual light. He is the spiritual light, which leads Believers through the darkness of this world and the world to come. Jehovah Ori, the Lord our light is a great name of God for Believers to hold on to, particularly, in the last moments of life. God our light, also helps his people in times of trials and temptation.

There are times and seasons of life, when the storms and challenges of life rage, and people suffer hardships and afflictions of life. These are tough times, when Believers should call on the name of the Lord our Light, who can shine his light in the darkness, and walk with them through the valleys of the journeys of life, comforting and showing them the way. God our Light is a comforter, light supplies comfort, warmth, peace, and protection from fear and worry. The knowledge that God is light, offers Believers hope and serves as a battle cry against the enemy and his forces of darkness.

> "Rejoice not against me, O my enemy, when I fall, I shall arise, when I sit in darkness, the Lord shall be a light on to me."
>
> Micah 7:8

God covers his people with his glory, thereby, giving them his light. His glory shines forth light and brings beauty and splendour to the people of God.

> "No longer will the sun be your light by day, nor the brightness of the moon shine on your night, for the Lord will be your everlasting light, and your God will be your splendour."
>
> Isaiah 60:19

God expects his people to shine brightly and be the light of the world. The Bible states God brought Believers from darkness into his marvellous light.

> "But you are a chosen people, a royal priesthood, a holy nation, God's special possession, that you may declare the praises of him, who called you out of darkness, into his wonderful light."
>
> 1 Peter 2:9

Jesus said he and the people of God are the light of the world.

> "You are the light of the world."
>
> Matthew 5:14

> "I am the light of the world, whosoever follows me, will not walk in darkness, but will have the light of life."
>
> John 8:12

Therefore, Believers in Christ Jesus ought to walk in the light of the word of God. The truth of the word of God brings light and helps Christians in the path of righteousness, holiness, and truth.

> "Your word is a lamp to my feet, and a light to my path."
>
> Psalm 119:105

PRAYER

The Lord our Light, we give you thanks, that you shine your light, on the world. Thank you for penetrating the darkness and giving us light. We thank you, for your glory that gives us beauty and splendour in Jesus' name. Amen.

CHAPTER 20

JEHOVAH GOELEKH - THE LORD OUR REDEEMER

"This is what the Lord says, your Redeemer, the Holy One of Israel: I am the LORD your God, who teaches you what is best for you, who directs you in the way you should go."

ISAIAH 48:17

The word redeem means an act conducted to compensate for wrongdoing or an act of terror, atonement for sin to make amends for wrongdoing, or an error. A Redeemer saves the redeemed from punishment, redemption requires an exchange of some kind. The Bible explains the blood of Jesus paid for the wages of sin. The gospel says the wages of sin is death. So, to avoid the damnation of the human soul to hell after death, God gave his only Son, Jesus Christ to die for the sin of disobedience committed by the first man, Adam (Genesis 2:4-3:24).

> "When Adam sinned, sin entered the world. Adam's sin brought death, so death spread to everyone, for everyone sinned."
>
> Romans 5:12

To the unbelievers, this principle of ascribing one man's sin of disobedience to every human being, even babies who seem innocent and without sin or the ability to sin, is difficult to understand. The biblical truth is that humanity has sinned and fallen short of God's glory, because everyone who is born of the seed of Adam, is conceived with his corrupt seed. So, everyone has therefore, inherited Adam's sin and are born corrupt and imperfect.

> "Surely, I was sinful at birth, sinful from the time my mother conceived me."
>
> Psalm 51:5

The good news, therefore, is that those who are reborn in Christ Jesus (Born Again Christians) are born of his incorruptible seed because Jesus was born by the immaculate conception (without man's sexual intercourse). God the Holy Spirit overshadowed his mother the Virgin Mary to avoid the contamination of the sinful genes of the Adamic man. Those who are born again are considered without sin and obtain salvation, because they have the fatherhood of God the Father, through their connection with his Son Jesus Christ.

> "So, in Christ Jesus, you are all children of God through faith."
>
> Galatians 3:26

> "Having been born again, not of corruptible seed but incorruptible, through the word of God which lives and abides forever."
>
> 1 Peter 1:23

> "But there is a significant difference between Adam's sin and God's gracious gift. For the sin of this one man, Adam brought death to many. But even greater is God's wonderful grace and his gift of forgiveness to many through this other man, Jesus Christ."
>
> Romans 5:15

Jesus introduced the principle of humanity's need to be born again for salvation to occur in his conversation with a certain Pharisees named Nicodemus, a ruler of the Jew (John 3). Jesus explained to Nicodemus what the concept of being born again is all about. A person must give their life to God the Father with faith in Christ Jesus through the power of the Holy Spirit. He also confirmed the importance of water baptism.

THE CONCEPT OF BORN AGAIN

> "This man came to Jesus by night and said to him, Rabbi, we know that you are a teacher come from God, for no one can do these signs that you do unless God is with him. Jesus answered and said to him, most assuredly, I say to you unless one is born again, he cannot see the kingdom of God. Nicodemus said to him: How can a man be born when he is old?

Can he enter a second time into his mother's womb and be born? Jesus answered, most assuredly I say to you, unless one is born of water and the Spirit, he cannot enter the Kingdom of God. That which is born of the flesh is flesh, and that which is born of the Spirit is spirit."

John 3:2-6

It is refreshing and encouraging to know God is a redeeming Father, whose measure of love is the life of his Son, Jesus Christ. God through the death of his Son Jesus Christ, redeemed the soul of whoever believes in him. He purchased their lost soul with the blood of his Son Jesus Christ (Galatians 3:13). Jesus saved humanity from the sin of disobedience, which calls for spiritual death. He died and rose from the dead, and he lives forever. And because he lives, Believers in Christ Jesus will also receive eternal life from God. The Lord the Redeemer redeems all those who call to him to save them.

"For in Adam, all die, so in Christ, all will be made alive."

1 Corinthians 15:22

PRAYER

Dear Lord, Our Redeemer, we ask that you give illumination of your word to those who do not yet know you as their Father and Redeemer, in Jesus' name. Amen.

CHAPTER 21

ELOHIM MACHESLANU - GOD OUR REFUGE

"My salvation and my honour, rest on God my strong rock, and my refuge. Trust in him always, O people, pour out your hearts before him. God is our refuge."

PSALM 62:7-8

A refuge is a place of safety and security, God is known as a God who offers refuge for his people. Believers dwell safely, securely, and peacefully in God their Refuge. The name of God Our Refuge is a useful name for those who fear God and put their trust in him for protection. Believers depend on God as their refuge in times of trouble or tribulation in their lives or the world at large, such as physical wars, pandemics (disease outbreaks) or spiritual warfare. However, it is only those who fear God and take their refuge in him, that can find refuge in God.

"In the fear of the Lord is strong confidence and his children shall have a place of refuge."

Proverbs 14:26

The name God our Refuge is packed with promises such as the benefits of safety and protection. Psalm 91 gives a comprehensive detail of the benefits of making God a refuge which is a matter of choice.

Psalm 91

"**Whoever** dwells in the shelter, of the Highest will rest in the shadow of the Almighty. I will say of the Lord, He is my refuge and my fortress, my God, in whom I trust. Surely, he will save you from the fowler's snare and the deadly pestilence.

He will cover you with his feathers, and under his wings, you will find refuge; his faithfulness will be your shield and rampart. You will not fear the terror of night, nor the arrow that flies by day, nor the pestilence that stalks in the darkness, nor the plague that destroys at midday. A thousand may fall at your side, ten thousand at your right hand, but it will not come near you. You will only observe with your eyes and see the punishment of the wicked. If you say, the Lord is my refuge, and you make the Highest your dwelling, no harm will overtake you, no disaster will come near your tent.

For he will command his angels concerning you to guard you in all your ways; they will lift you in their hands so that you will not strike your foot against a stone. You will tread on the lion and the cobra; you will trample the great lion and the serpent.

Because he loves me, says the Lord, I will rescue him; I will protect him, for he acknowledges my name. He will call on me, and I will answer him; I will be with him in trouble, I will deliver him and honour him. With long life, I will satisfy him, and show him my salvation."

Psalm 91:1-16

The invitation of safekeeping is open to all of humanity. However, Psalm 91 emphasised the importance of individuals choosing to seek God for his protection, by choosing to dwell in his shelter to qualify for his safety and refuge. The psalm says whoever dwells in God's shelter will find rest under his protective arms. Christians should, therefore, develop the habit of making God their refuge by having faith and trust in God our refuge. The promise is for those who are willing and obedient.

PRAYER

O Lord our refuge, we thank you for your protective nature over your people. We thank you for your care, we pray to live safely in your secret place in Jesus' name. Amen.

Chapter 22

El Meleki - God Our King

"I will exalt you, my God and King. I will bless your name forever and ever. Every day, I will bless you. I will praise your name forever and ever."

PSALM 145:1-2

A King is a ruler of a state, but God is the ruler of the whole universe. God is the creator of everything, he has sovereignty over human life, kings, rulers, judges, and the wealth of the nations. God the King rules in the affairs of men, he has power and the right to assign his rulership to whosoever he wishes on earth.

"The decision is announced by messengers, the holy one declares the verdict, so that the living may know that the Highest is sovereign over all kingdoms on earth and gives them to anyone he wishes and sets over them the lowliest of people."

Daniel 4:17

The Bible declares God is the King of Kings (Revelation 19:16). He sent his Son Jesus as king, and declares, he should be worshipped (Psalm 2).

"The Lord sits enthroned over the flood; the Lord is enthroned as King forever."

Psalm 29:10

The triumphal entry of the Lord Jesus Christ, into Jerusalem before the last supper, displayed the glory of his Sonship and Kingship on earth.

"Tell, the people of Jerusalem: Look, your King is coming to you. He is humble, riding on a donkey, riding on a donkey's colt."

Matthew 21:5

The fact that God is our King, gives joy and gladness to his people. The Book of Psalms contains a lot of praises to God.

"The Lord reigns, let the earth be glad, let the distant shores rejoice."

Psalm 97:1

A Psalm of Praise of David

"I will exalt you, my God the King, I will praise your name forever and ever. Every day, I will praise you and extol your name forever and ever. Great is the Lord and most worthy of praise; his greatness no one can fathom."

Psalm 145:1-3

PRAYER

God Our King, we worship you, our Eternal King. "Now to the King eternal, immortal, invisible, the only God, be honour and glory forever and ever (1 Timothy 1:17)." Amen.

Chapter 23

El Nekamoth - The God Who Avenges

> *"He is the God who avenges me, who subdues nations under me."*
>
> **PSALM 18:47**

To avenge means to inflict harm or injury in return for a wrong done to oneself. The word also means to take revenge for an offence committed against one. The Bible warns the people of God never to embark on any form of revenge against wrongdoers because it is God who avenges them.

> "Do not seek revenge or bear a grudge against any of your people but love your neighbour as yourself. I am the Lord."
>
> Leviticus 19:18

God promises to avenge his people because revenge is a complicated emotion that often ends in pain. Revenge creates the negative emotion of hatred which can thwart the loving purpose that God needs from his people. Whenever human beings, devise their plans for revenge, there is a tendency to make mistakes, harm others, commit sinful acts, become bitter, or hateful. People in search of revenge have been known to become despicable, thereby, falling out of love into the evil sin of wickedness. The vengeful act is contrary to the act of mercy and love commanded by God.

> "But I say to you, love your enemies and pray for those who persecute you."
>
> Matthew 5:44

A person in search of punishment for a wrongdoer, cannot forgive or love their enemies. God in his infinite wisdom knows, there is a risk of a revengeful human soul becoming twisted, mischievous, and evil in the process of taking revenge on their enemies. The Bible teaches Christians to be forgiving, so Believers should let go and let the God who avenges take revenge on their behalf. God who avenges knows best, he will repay and compensate his people.

> "If it is possible on your part, live at peace with everyone. Do not avenge yourselves beloved, leave room for God's wrath. For it is written, vengeance is mine. I will repay says the Lord."
>
> Romans 12:18-19

Hence, the godly way to manage an offence is to commit the wrong to God in prayer. Vengeance belongs to God, he will avenge.

"Vengeance is mine; I will repay in due time their foot will slip for the day of disaster is near and their doom is coming quickly."

Deuteronomy 32:35

> ## PRAYER
> *Lord who avenges, we say thank you, that you avenge your people.*

CHAPTER 24

Jehovah Selai - The Lord Our Rock

"He sang: The Lord is my rock, fortress, and my saviour, my God is my rock, in whom I find protection. He is my shield, the power that saves me and the place of my safety. He is my refuge, my saviour, the one who saves me from violence."

2 SAMUEL 22:2-3

The above scripture was the song of deliverance David sang when God delivered and saved him from the hands of his enemy King Saul. God the Rock confirms God is a protector, upon whom, Believers stand safe and secure. Believers, have hope, they will never fail, be consumed, or be defeated by their enemies because God is their Rock and Refuge. The Lord the Rock protects his people who call upon him to save them.

The Bible declares Believers will never be shaken or afraid when they trust in the Lord their Rock, the horn of their salvation. Whatever comes their way, they will not be moved because God is their rock, a solid foundation, the chief cornerstone that supports them. Therefore, Believers should not be moved by what they see, but by the revelation of the word of God.

> "He only is my rock and my salvation, he is my defence, I shall not be moved."
>
> Psalm 62:6

> "Therefore, this is what the Sovereign Lord says, look, I am placing a foundation stone in Jerusalem, a firm and tested stone. It is a precious cornerstone that is safe to build on. Whoever believes need never be shaken."
>
> Isaiah 28:16, Romans 9:33

The church of God is built upon the Lord our Rock. The Bible affirms the gates of hell will never prevail against the church because it is set up and built on the revelation of Jesus being the saviour which is the foundational truth of the gospel.

> "Now I say to you that you are Peter (which means rock) and upon this rock, I will build my church, and all the powers of hell will not conquer it."
>
> Matthew 16:18

A rock in biblical terms symbolises solidity, stability, and durability. The name the Lord our Rock, illustrates the strength of

God as being strong, durable, with a nature of consistency, and firmness. He is dependable, faithful, and never fails to perform his word or save his people (1 Corinthians 1:9). He is the Rock upon which Believers stand or hide for protection and safety especially those who listen to the word of God and obey them. Jesus and the revelation of the word of God, the Bible is the rock upon which Believers must build their faith. Jesus said:

> "Anyone who listens to my teaching and follows it is wise, like a person who builds a house on solid rock."
>
> Matthew 7:24

Paul spoke of Jesus being the chief cornerstone that supports the Christian Faith.

> "Together, we are his house, built on the foundation of the apostles and the prophets. And the cornerstone is Christ Jesus himself."
>
> Ephesians 2:20

PRAYER

O Lord, our rock, we thank you for your word and revelation that is our stability. We trust you and stand upon your solid foundation that can never be shaken. Thank you for being our stronghold, our tower, and our rock in Jesus' name. Amen.

Chapter 25

Elohim Azar - God Our Helper

"Behold, God is my helper, the Lord is the upholder of my life."

Psalm 54:4

Elohim Azar means God is our helper. A helper is someone who helps others who need their help. The name speaks of God's strength and power, and his ability to supply protection, helping hand, provision, and peace to his people. God is a helper who upholds and supports a secure life for whoever puts their trust in him. Christians, serve a Living God, who helps his people live a winning and secure life if they dare to ask him for help. The Bible declares the people of God are overcomers because God is their helper.

"There is no one like the God of Israel. He rides across the heavens to help you, across the skies in his majesty."

Deuteronomy 33:26

"The Lord is on my side. He is my helper; therefore, I will look in triumph on those who hate me."

Psalm 118:7

Believers should have faith in the God who helps because he alone can uphold and keep them above the enemy. He is always ready and available to help and deliver his people from trouble, so Believers need not fear the enemy or the challenges of life.

"God is our refuge and strength always ready to help in times of trouble."

Psalm 46:1

"Fear not, for I am with you, be not afraid for I am your God. I will strengthen you. Yes, I will help you! Yes, I will uphold you with the right hand of my righteousness."

Isaiah 41:10

PRAYER

We pray O Lord that you will be our helper in times of trouble, because of your help, we will fear no evil in Jesus' name. Amen.

CHAPTER 26

JEHOVAH NISSI - THE LORD OUR BANNER

"After the defeat of the Amalekites, Moses built an altar and named it the Lord is my banner."

EXODUS 17:15

Jehovah Nissi means the Lord our banner. The term banner is a sign that unifies people on the battlefield. It symbolises confidence in God as a protector, shield, and defender. The name was given by Moses to God when he built an altar of praise and thanksgiving to celebrate the Lord's help in the Israelites' defeat of the Amalekites, at Rephidim, during their battles to take possession of their promised land (Exodus 17:15).

Christians, have an advantage in warfare because Jehovah Nissi is their defence and protector. Spiritually, Believers display this name over their lives and possessions, declaring to the enemy that God is with his people in battle, to defend and help them conquer every enemy. The Bible states God's love is a banner over his people, and he gives a banner to those who fear him.

> "But you have raised a banner for those who fear you, a rallying point in the face of attack.
>
> Psalm 60:4

> "Let him lead me to the banquet hall and let his banner over me be love."
>
> Song of Solomon 2:4

PRAYER

The Lord God our Jehovah Nissi, we thank you for your daily protection over your people. Guard and protect us today and forever and let your banner over them be your love in Jesus' name. Amen.

CHAPTER 27

JEHOVAH RAPHA - THE LORD WHO HEALS

"Moses said if you listen carefully to the voice of the Lord your God and do what is right in his eyes and pay attention to his commands and keep all his statutes, then I will not bring on you the diseases I inflicted on the Egyptians, for I am the Lord who heals you."

EXODUS 15:26

As human beings who live in a fallen world, we are vulnerable to sicknesses and diseases. So, Christians ought to trust in Jehovah Rapha, the God who heals. Believers, understand the fact that God heals diseases supernaturally and sometimes through the wisdom of medical science. The Bible states, Believers, are healed by the stripes of Jesus Christ, his chastisement saved humankind from sin and sickness.

The Christian doctrine teaches Believers received divine healing and salvation at the time of Jesus' death. Redemption and healing became complete at the resurrection of Christ Jesus. According to the Gospel of John, Pontius Pilate, the Roman governor of Judea, ordered Jesus to be flogged. The Roman soldiers beat Jesus with a lead-tipped whip, he was beaten and crowned with thorns, on his way to crucifixion by the Romans. He shed blood, which Christians believe gave them healing and divine health. The work of healing was completed at the death and resurrection of Jesus Christ.

Believers believe they obtain supernatural healing by the blood of Jesus. They believe there is healing, peace, and wholeness in Jesus Christ, the Lord who heals. Therefore, Christians declare: "By his stripes we are healed" to claim their healing and divine health.

> "But he was wounded for our transgressions, he was bruised for our iniquities, the chastisement of our peace was upon him, and by his stripes, we are healed."
>
> Isaiah 53:5

God desires that Believers live in divine health if they keep his commandments. Apostle John, the author of the Bible book of John prayed:

The Prayer of John for Health and Prosperity

> "Beloved, I pray that you prosper in all things, and be in health, just as your soul prospers."
>
> 3 John 1:2

Christians enjoy divine health and God's divine protection from illnesses if they remain in God. Psalm 91 states God protects his people from pestilence and plagues because he is their refuge and healer.

> ## PRAYER
> *O Lord God, our Healer, we thank you for your healing grace and the promise of divine health. We ask that you heal those who are sick in Jesus' name. Amen.*

Chapter 28

Emmanuel - God is With Us

"Therefore, the Lord himself will give you a sign. Behold, the virgin will be with child and will give birth to a son and will call him Emmanuel."

ISAIAH 7:14

Emmanuel means God is with us. Isaiah prophesied of the coming Messiah whose name will be called Emmanuel (Isaiah 7:14). The prophecy was fulfilled by the birth of the Lord Jesus Christ whom `Christians believe is the child, Emmanuel. The angel of `the Lord appeared to Joseph the father of Jesus and instructed him to take Mary as his wife because the child conceived in her is from the Holy Spirit. He confirmed it took place to fulfil the prophecy in the Old Testament Bible.

"And it took place to fulfil what the Lord had said through the prophet: The virgin will conceive and give birth, and they will call him Immanuel (which means God with us)."

Matthew 1:22-23

Emmanuel is a wonderful name of God because it reminds Believers of God's constant presence. God is omnipresent, he is everywhere, and he promised to be with Christians till the end of the world. Jesus asked his disciples to go and make disciples of all nations promising to be with them till the end of time.

> "Therefore, go and make disciples of all nations, baptising them in the name of the Father and the Son, and of the Holy Spirit, and teaching them to obey everything I have commanded you. And surely, I am with you always, to the very end of the age."

Matthew 28:19-20

The knowledge that God is with his people gives strength and courage. Knowing God is with Believers should empower them to proclaim the gospel with boldness as instructed by God. Christians should be assured of God being with them because they serve Emmanuel – God is with us. They triumph over evil and wickedness because God is with them to protect and support them. When the enemy comes against them, they know God is with us, will protect and help them overcome. When God is with us, no one can contend against Believers because greater is he that is in them, than the one in the world. Believers are overcomers in Christ Jesus.

> "But you belong to God, my dear children. You have already won a victory over those people because the Spirit who lives in you is greater than the spirit who lives in the world."
>
> 1 John 4:4

> "Device a plan, but it will be thwarted. State a proposal, but it will not happen for God is with us."
>
> Isaiah 8:10

Once a person becomes a child of God (Born Again Christian) they qualify for the presence of the Holy Spirit who lives in them. Jesus promised to ask God the Father to give Believers the Holy Spirit after he departs for heaven to help them live a successful Christian life.

> "And I will ask the Father, and he will give you another Helper (Comforter, Advocate, Intercessor, Counsellor, Strengthener, and Standby) to be with you forever."
>
> John 14:16

PRAYER

O Lord, we thank you for your presence in our lives. You are the light and the hope of the world, without Jesus, humankind will be lost, so, we ask you to fill the world with your presence, in Jesus' name, we pray. Amen.

CHAPTER 29

El Olam - The Everlasting God

*"Abraham planted a tamarisk tree in
Beersheba and there he called on the name
of the Lord, the Everlasting God."*

GENESIS 21:33

El Olam means the Everlasting God or simply the Eternal God. People in the Bible have a common habit of celebrating their wins with a prayer of thanksgiving to God, using new names to praise him. Abraham worshipped God with the names El Olam, the Everlasting God after he entered a treaty of peace with Abimelech and Phicol the commander of the Philistine army.

Abimelech approached Abraham saying the Lord was with him in everything he did because he was prospering in the land of the Philistines, so he asked Abraham to be kind to him and the Philistines. After the treaty at Beersheba, Abraham asked him to restore the well of water seized by his servants. To celebrate the covenant of peace, Abraham worshipped the Lord with the name, Everlasting God.

> "After making their covenant at Beersheba, Abimelech left with Phicol, the commander of his army, and they returned home to the land of the Philistines. Then Abraham planted a tamarisk tree at Beersheba, and there he worshipped the Lord the Eternal God."
>
> Genesis 21:32-33

El Olam means the Everlasting God because the word 'Olam' means forever or always, it refers to God who is eternal and never dies. God has no end because he is the Alpha and Omega - The Beginning and the End. The scriptures confirm the Lord will reign forever with no end.

> "The Lord reigns forever and ever."
>
> Exodus 15:18

> "Before the mountains were born or you brought forth the earth and the world, from everlasting to everlasting you are God."
>
> Psalm 90:2

PRAYER

O Lord, the Everlasting Father, we call upon your name, the Eternal God, we ask you to abide with us forever in Jesus' name. Amen.

Chapter 30

Jehovah Eloheeka - The Lord Our God

"Then God gave the people all these instructions: I am the Lord your God, who rescued you from the land of Egypt, out of the place of slavery."

EXODUS 20:1-2

The name the Lord our God, expresses the supreme nature of God. He is the sovereign God who has the ultimate power to save. God is true to his word, he delivered the Israelites with a display of his formidable power through the affliction of plagues sent to the Egyptians, the enemies of his people. When he gave them the ten commandments, he reminded them that he is their God who delivered and saved them from their oppressors.

In this same manner, God saved all of humanity from the sin of disobedience. He gave up his son Jesus Christ to die for the atonement for sin, so, Jesus became our Lord and Saviour. Christians should, therefore, keep God's commandment by loving him and their neighbours because the Lord is God.

> ## PRAYER
> *The Lord our God, we give you thanks. We declare you as our Lord God and saviour. Keep us as the sheep of your pasture in Jesus' name. Amen.*

Chapter 31

Jehovah Maozi - The Lord Our Strength

"God is our refuge and strength, an ever-present help in times of trouble."

PSALM 46:1

Strength means the quality or state of being mentally, emotionally, financially, or spiritually strong. God is strong and powerful; the Bible proclaims: "Blessed are those whose strength is God" (Psalm 84:5). God gives his people strength for everyday living, he promised to renew their strength like the eagle.

> "But those who trust in the Lord will find new strength. They will soar high on wings like eagles. They will run and not grow weary. They will walk and not faint."
>
> Isaiah 40:31

God gives his people strength; they go from strength to strength (Psalm 84:7) because God is their strength. Christians should remember that God is their strength and declare so daily. That way, they will rest in the Lord of Strength, live in peace, and rejoice in his salvation.

> "The Lord will give strength to his people and bless them with peace."
>
> Psalm 29:11

Believers lacking in strength can ask God our Strength to strengthen them, because God is the source of human strength. Samson a man of great strength in the Bible depended on God for his strength. When he lacked strength, he prayed to ask God for strength and God renewed his strength (Judges 16). The Bible records he killed more men in his later days than his former to avenge his eyes, which was plucked out by the Philistines.

THE PRAYER OF SAMSON FOR STRENGTH

> "Then Samson prayed to the Lord, Sovereign Lord, remember me again. O God, please strengthen me just one more time. With one blow, let me pay back the Philistines for the loss of my two eyes. Then Samson put his hands on the pillars that held up the temple.
>
> Pushing against them with both hands, he prayed: Let me die with the Philistines. And the temple crashed down on the Philistine rulers and all the

people. So, he killed more people when he died than he had during his entire lifetime."

Judges 16:28-30

PRAYER

Sovereign Lord God our strength, we thank you for being our strength. We pray that you strengthen us and renew our strength like the eagle in Jesus' name.' Amen.
God is your Strength!

CHAPTER 32

JEHOVAH ELOHEENU - THE LORD OUR GOD

"Hear O Israel, the Lord Our God, the Lord is one."

DEUTERONOMY 6:4

The name Jehovah Eloheenu is like Jehovah Eloheka. Jehovah Eloheenu means the Lord our God. The names inform Christians of the scriptural truth that God is a Father to his people. Therefore, Believers, have the right to call God Father.

The good news of the gospel message says God has adopted Believers into his Kingdom. He has given those who believe and put their faith in his Son Jesus Christ, the right to call him their God. God is the Lord of his adopted people; he is titled the King of Kings and the Lord of Lords.

"The spirit you received does not make you slaves so that you live in fear again, rather, the Spirit you received brought about your adoption to sonship. And by him, we cry "Abba, Father."

Romans 8:15

> ## PRAYER
> *O Lord our God, we thank you for the privilege to call you father. We will forever be thankful for your grace. We ask that you keep us hidden and protected in your love in Jesus' name. Amen.*

Chapter 33

Jehovah Hoseenu - The Lord Our Maker

"O come let us worship and bow down. Let us kneel before the Lord our maker."

PSALM 95:6

Jehovah Hoseenu is one of the names of God that inform us of our creator's identity. God is the creator of heaven and the earth. The Bible gives an account of how God created human beings.

> "Then God said, let us make man in our image, according to our likeness, and let them rule over the fish of the sea and the birds of the sky and the cattle and all the earth, and over every creeping thing that creeps on the earth. So, God created man in his

image, in the image of God he created them, male and female he created them."

Genesis 1:26-27

God created humankind, contrary to human speculations on creation such as Evolution and the Big Bang theories that say otherwise. Biblical record makes it clear that God is the creator of all things including human beings and every living thing. There are Bible verses about the fact that God created man and he is our maker.

"I have made the earth, the men and the beasts which are on the face of the earth by my great power and by my outstretched arm, and I will give it to the one who is pleasing in my sight."

Jeremiah 27:5

"Know that the Lord himself is God, it is he who has made us, and not we, we are his people and the sheep of his pasture."

Psalm 100:3

"Thus says God the Lord, who created the heavens and stretched them out, who spread out the earth and its offspring, who gives breath to the people on it and spirit to those who walk in it."

Isaiah 42:5

"For your maker is your husband. The Lord Almighty is his name. The holy one of Israel is your redeemer. He is called the God of all earth."

Isaiah 54:5

PRAYER

O Lord God our maker, we adore and bless your holy name. We honour you, God our Maker, in Jesus' name. Amen.

Chapter 34

Jehovah Shalom - The Lord Our Peace

> *"The Lord said to him. Peace be with you. Do not be afraid for you will not die. So, Gideon built an altar to the Lord there and called it The Lord Is Peace. To this day it stands in Ophrah of Abiezrites"*
>
> **JUDGES 6:23-24**

Shalom is a common salutation used by Israelites to greet one another. The word Shalom means peace, which Christians refer to as "nothing broken - nothing missing" (fullness of peace) that signifies wholeness, completeness, and peace. Peace is a state of tranquillity or freedom from disturbance.

The name Jehovah Shalom came from Gideon in the Book of Judges. When God asked him to deliver the Israelites from the Midianites' oppression, he became afraid, so, God comforted and encouraged him. Gideon in appreciation of God's encouragement that brought him peace of mind built an altar of thanksgiving to the Lord who comforted him, and blessed him with the new name Jehovah Shalom, meaning the Lord is Peace.

Christians of old celebrated God with new names, whenever he did wonderful things for them that made them glad. Christians of today will be blessed if they learn to glorify God with creative new names. Prophet Isaiah prophesied about the God of Peace.

> "For a child will be born to us, a son will be given to us, and the government will rest on his shoulders. And his name will be called Wonderful Counsellor, Mighty God, Eternal Father, Prince of Peace."
>
> Isaiah 9:6

True to the prophecy, Jesus was born as the Prince of Peace who comforts the people of God and give his people peace that surpasses all understanding. Jehovah Shalom comforts Believers and rids them of anxiety and stress. God gives his people peace and strength (Psalm 29:11). He keeps them from fearing evil and helps them dwell safely and securely.

> "And the peace of God, surpassing all understanding, will guard your hearts and your minds in Christ Jesus."
>
> Philippians 4:7

The question is how do we enter the peace of God? First, we must understand, the meaning of peace being a quiet state of mind, a spiritual blessedness that only God can provide. Peace is a serene state of mind free from troubles that true Believers alone can enjoy when they enter the rest of God in faith, knowing God is their strength and trusting completely in him. Peace is therefore, achieved by trusting and obeying God and his word. The Bible states there is a special sabbath rest available to Christians who trust in God (Hebrews 4:9).

Fear, rebellion, hardening of heart, doubt, anxiety, sin, and disobedience are notable examples that prevent human beings from entering the peace of God. The Israelites, despite the miracles they witnessed God perform for them, remained in disobedience to God and served other gods, so God punished them and banned them from entering his rest.

> "So, I was angry with that generation, I said their hearts are always going astray, and they have not known my ways. So, in my anger I took an oath, they will never enter my place of rest"
>
> Hebrews 3:10-11

> "God's promise of entering his rest still stands, so we ought to tremble with fear that some of you might fail to experience it."
>
> Hebrews 4:1

Psalm 23 teaches how to walk in the peace of God. The key is to trust and obey God as our Shepherd. When Believers trust God, they enjoy Shalom, a life of peace free from fear, stress, or worries.

PRAYER

Lord our Peace, we pray that you be with every Believer in Christ. We ask you to grant them peace in Jesus' name. Amen.

Chapter 35

Jehovah Yisrael - The God of Israel

> *"God said to Moses: Say to the people of Israel, the Lord the God of your fathers the God of Abraham, the God of Isaac, and the God of Jacob has sent me to you. This is my name forever, the name you shall call me from generation to generation."*
>
> EXODUS 3:15

The God of Israel is the name that shows the nationality by which God initially associated himself with human beings. Christianity teaches God in the beginning, chose the people of Israel as his covenant people. He later, extended redemption to all of humanity, through his Son Jesus Christ. Zachariah the father of John the Baptist, blessed the God of Israel saying:

"Blessed is the Lord, the God of Israel because he has visited and provided redemption for his people."

Luke 1:68

PRAYER

"Praise be to the Lord, the God of Israel, from everlasting to everlasting. Amen and amen."
Psalm 41:13

Chapter 36

Jehovah Shammah - The Lord is There

> *"All the way around shall be eighteen thousand cubits. And the name of the city from that day shall be: THE LORD IS THERE"*
>
> **EZEKIEL 48:35**

God gave the name Jehovah Shammah to the future restored new Jerusalem. Prophet Ezekiel revealed his vision of the glory of the new Jerusalem in the Book of Ezekiel. Jehovah Shammah informs us of the presence of God in a place. Emmanuel is the presence of God with his people, Jehovah Shammah is God's presence in places.

Jehovah Shammah is a useful name to pray in times of loneliness, whenever Believers are on a journey away from home. A notable example is the experience of Jacob, who fled from home, after deceiving his brother Esau and cheating him of their father's firstborn blessing. He was lonely and afraid, he slept and dreamt of a ladder going up from earth to heaven at a place called Bethel.

In the vision, Jacob saw the angels of the Lord going up and down the stairway, above it, stood the Lord who spoke and blessed him. Jacob felt the presence of God at Bethel, Believers named the experience and place - The God of Bethel. God promised Jacob his presence will go with him wherever he goes.

> "Behold, I am with you and will keep you wherever you go and bring you back to this land. For I will not leave you until I have done what I have promised you."
>
> Genesis 28:15

> "When Jacob awoke from his sleep, he thought, surely the Lord is in this place, and I was not aware of it."
>
> Genesis 28:16

When God is in a place, there is security, safety, and peace. The Lord is here is a name Believers should proclaim in times of anxiety, loneliness, and uncertainties of life. Whatever the storms of life may bring, or wherever life takes the people of God, they should declare that the Lord is there!

Christians carry the presence of God, which is encouraging because God's presence brings his people rest. Moses enjoyed the presence of God; he did not go anywhere unless the presence of God went with him. He had a good relationship with Jehovah Shammah, which is described, in the Book of Exodus. Moses asked God to go with him and the people of Israel in their journey of life.

> "The Lord replied, my presence will go with you, and I will give you rest.
>
> Then Moses said to him, if your Presence does not go with us, do not send us up from here. How will anyone know that you are pleased with me and with your people unless you go with us? What else will distinguish me and your people from all the other people on the face of the earth?"
>
> Exodus 33:14-16

The presence of God brings joy, the Book of Psalms declares:

> "You make known to me the path of life, in your presence, there is fullness of joy, at your right hand, are pleasures forevermore."
>
> Psalm 16:11

Jehovah Shammah confirms the omnipresence and omnipotence power of God. He is present everywhere; his presence fills the heavens and the earth. And he promises never to leave or forsake his people (Hebrews 13:5). God is there, summarises the comfort, that knowing the name brings to Believers, especially in the darkest moments of life, knowing God is there is reassuring and inspiring for his people.

> "Even though I walk through the valley of the shadow of death, I will fear no evil, for you are with me, your rod, and your staff, they comfort me."
>
> Psalm 23:4

PRAYER

Dear Lord Jehovah Shammah, we thank you for your divine presence, thank you for your presence that brings comfort and peace. Amen.

Chapter 37

I AM - I AM Who I AM

"Then Moses asked God, suppose, I go to the Israelites, and say to them, the God of your fathers has sent me to you, and they ask me what his name is. What should I tell them? God said to Moses, I am who I am. This is what you are to say to the Israelites, I am, has sent me to you."

EXODUS 3:13-14

The name I AM means I AM Who I AM, or I AM That I AM which refers to God's ability to adapt or be adapted to many different functions or activities. The name speaks of the power and authority of God the creator. God revealed himself to Moses during his divine encounter with God at the burning bush as I AM. The name stands for the greatness of God, and his versatile nature to be whosoever he chooses to be. What a wonderful and impressive name!

I AM Who I AM is one of the greatest names of God because it meets every human need. The God I AM is a healer, provider, protector, saviour, or whatever his people ask him to be to them. The name connotes the confidence of God in his power and status as the Almighty God. I AM, reveals the omniscient and omnipotent nature of God. He is powerful and he knows all things, so, he can do all things especially those his people request from him according to his divine will.

I AM who I AM is an all-sufficient God, the name seems to declare that God's grace is sufficient for every human need. In God, we have provision, protection, joy, peace, deliverance, and salvation. I AM, delivered the people of Israel from bondage and slavery. The same God can save and deliver every Believer from their bondage and challenges of life. Believers must know, therefore, that in all circumstances they are more than conquerors in Christ Jesus.

> "My grace is sufficient for you, for my power is made perfect in weakness."
>
> 2 Corinthians 12:9

PRAYER

Almighty God the I AM Who I AM, we bless your glorious all-fulfilling, and all-satisfying name. We ask that you reveal your goodness to us in all aspects of life. Lord, the I am who I am, be sufficient for all our needs in Jesus' name. Amen.

Chapter 38

Jehovah Tsidkenu - The Lord Our Righteousness

> *"Behold the days are coming declares the Lord when I will raise for David a righteous branch and he will reign wisely as king and will administer justice and righteousness in the land. In his days, Judah will be saved, and Israel will dwell securely. And this is his name by which he will be called: The Lord Our Righteousness."*
>
> **JEREMIAH 23:5-6**

The Lord our righteousness is pure and holy, and in him, there is no sin, evil, or fault. The word righteous is the quality of being morally right or justified. It is simply the virtue of goodness and piety. God the Righteous God became the redeemer of human beings, through his righteousness, Believers become righteous. Jesus had no sin, so he was fit to become the sacrificial lamb who was killed to atone for the sin of humankind.

> "And you know that he was manifested to take away our sins, and in him is no sin."
>
> 1 John 3:5

Therefore, righteousness is given to Christians through the righteousness of Christ Jesus.

> "But now apart from the law the righteousness of God has been made known, to which the Law and Prophets testify. This righteousness is given through faith in Jesus Christ to all who believe. There is no difference between Jew and Gentile."
>
> Romans 3:21-22

God gives his righteousness freely to whosoever believes in his Son Jesus Christ. The way to righteousness, therefore, is not a good character or behaviour but faith in God.

> "Surely shall one say, in the Lord, have I righteousness and strength, even to him shall men come and all that are incensed against him shall be ashamed."
>
> Isaiah 45:24

Therefore, Believers must reach out in faith for the righteousness of Christ Jesus, through which they can live safely in peace, obtaining everlasting life in him.

"In those days shall Judah be saved, and Jerusalem shall dwell safely, and this is the name by which she shall be called: The Lord our righteousness."

Jeremiah 33:16

PRAYER

O Lord our Righteousness, we give thanks for imputing righteousness on your people. Amen.

Chapter 39

Jehovah Shaphat - The Lord Our Judge

"For the Lord is our judge, the Lord is our lawgiver, the Lord king, it is he who will save us."

ISAIAH 33:22

God our Judge is our judge; he rules in the affairs of men with righteousness. He does right by his people, his judgment is fair and just. God will not withhold justice from his people, nor does he refrain from giving punishment to the wicked.

> "Far be it from you to do such a thing-to kill the righteous with the wicked, treating the righteous and the wicked alike. Far be it from you! Will not the Judge of all the earth do right?"
>
> Genesis 18:25

Our God does right by his people, so, Believers can freely take their grievances to him. God sees and knows all things; the Bible says he will repay his people and make recompense. He avenges his people by punishing the wicked and compensating the righteous.

PRAYER

Jehovah Shaphat, the Lord our Judge, we praise you for you are God of recompense, who judge people fairly. Amen.

Chapter 40

El Rachum - The Merciful God

"For the Lord, your God is merciful. He will not abandon or destroy you or forget the covenant with your fathers, which he swore to them by oath."

DEUTERONOMY 4:31

The Hebrew name of God El Rachum means the merciful or compassionate God in the English Language. The name shows the compassionate nature of God. Merciful is an adjective describing God's grace of mercy. A similar word is forgiving, which means to release someone who has offended you from punishment. Mercy is showing graciousness, it takes the grace of God for human beings to understand mercy, because they are not used to getting something for nothing. People are often, unable to comprehend the full meaning of the mercy of God, which is getting things they do not deserve; they think there is a catch somewhere.

God is Love, his loving devotion enables him to forgive people who deserve punishment. He treats all men equally; he shows mercy to those in distress even when they deserve suffering. Jesus' sermon on the mount instructs the people of God to show mercy to one another. God expects his people to live above bitterness and hate.

Therefore, Christians must be kind and merciful. The Bible promises a reward for those who show mercy to others.

> "Blessed are the merciful, for they will be shown mercy."
>
> Matthew 5:7

The word blessed means to be favoured by God and man. It implies a state of happiness, well-being, and joyfulness. An expression that holds a powerful state of divine joy and perfect happiness. So, when Christians imitate the Merciful God, we reap the benefit of overflowing joy and blessedness. Mercy is the spiritual blessedness of God; it comes with the gift of God's glory. Moses asked the Lord God to show him his glory, and God revealed to him his mercy and graciousness.

> "And the Lord passed before him and proclaimed. The Lord the Lord God, merciful and gracious, long-suffering, and abundant in goodness and truth."
>
> Exodus 34:6

God is a gracious God who has the character of patience and longsuffering. He shows his people mercy and offers forgiveness of sin to humankind even when they do not deserve such grace. God overlooks the wicked nature of human beings that began at the fall of Adam's sin of disobedience.

> "The Lord is longsuffering and of great mercy, forgiving iniquity and transgression, and by no means clearing the guilty, visiting the iniquity of the fathers upon the children unto the third and fourth generation."
>
> Numbers 14:18

From the preceding scripture, we get a word of caution that God, though merciful and longsuffering is a just Judge, who will judge his people according to their deeds. Apostle Paul taught Believers not to continue to live in sin with a false expectation that the grace of God will abound.

> "Well then, should we keep on sinning so that God can show us more and more of his wonderful grace? Of course not! Since we have died to sin, how can we continue to live in it."
>
> Romans 6:1-2

Therefore, Christians must learn to honour the Merciful God, and not take his merciful nature for granted. The Lord is good, his mercy endures forever, but his people must not take advantage of his compassion and continue in sin and wickedness. When Believers are obedient to God, it is no longer them who live but Christ in them. Christians get a new nature in Christ Jesus that requires an obedient and merciful living.

However, most human beings struggle with the concept of mercy. They cannot show mercy nor accept the merciful nature of God when demonstrated to people other than themselves. Whenever God shows mercy to people, certain individuals will selfishly get angry. The biblical story of the anger of Jonah is an excellent example that shows this human weakness.

God asked Jonah to preach against the people of Nineveh, but he fled from his calling. He quickly discovered God is an Omnipresent God when he caught up with him in the form of a storm at sea. God in his mercy kept him safe in the belly of a large fish. Afterwards, Jonah repented and went back to evangelise in the city of Nineveh as God instructed him. The people repented, so, God forgave them and relented from his anger and threat to wipe them out. But to Jonah this seemed very wrong. So, he became angry at God for forgiving and sparing them from punishment.

The Prayer of Jonah against God's Compassion:

"Jonah however was greatly displeased, and he became angry, so he prayed to the Lord saying: O Lord is this not what I said while I was still in my own country? Therefore, I was so quick to flee towards Tarshish. I knew that you are a gracious and compassionate God, slow to anger, abounding in loving devotion. One who relents in sending disaster. And now, O Lord, please take my life from me, for it is better for me to die than to live."

Jonah 4:1-3

God's Response to Jonah's Prayer and Complaints

"**But the Lord replied**: Is it right for you to be angry?

Jonah had gone out and sat down at a place east of the city. There he made himself a shelter, to see what would happen to the city. Then the Lord God provided a leafy plant and made it grow up over Jonah to ease his discomfort, and Jonah was very happy about the plant. But at dawn the next day God provided a worm which chewed the plant so that it withered.

When the sun rose, God provided a scorching east wind, and the sun blazed on Jonah's head so that he grew faint. He wanted to die, and said, it would be better for me to die than to live.

But God said to Jonah, is it right for you to be angry about the plant?

It is, he said. And I'm so angry I wish I were dead.

But the Lord said, you have been concerned about this plant, though you did not tend it or make it grow. It sprang up overnight and died overnight. And should I not have concern for the great city of Nineveh, in which there are more than a hundred and twenty thousand people who cannot tell their right hand from their left, and many animals?"

Jonah 4: 4-11

Jesus also taught on the unmerciful nature of human beings in the parable of the Unmerciful Servant (Matthew 18:21-35). In the story, Jesus in response to Peter's question of how many times he should forgive his brother or sister who sins against him, said forgiveness should be unlimited. Jesus gave a figure of seventy times seven and used the parable of the Unmerciful Servant to teach the disciples about the importance of mercy and forgiveness.

In the parable, Jesus said the kingdom of heaven is like a king who wanted to settle accounts with his servants. One of his servants, who owed him ten thousand bags of gold, was unable to pay, so, he forgave him and cancelled the debt, when he begged him to be patient with him.

However, the servant, did not forgive his fellow servant who owed him a debt of just a hundred silver coins, he had him thrown into prison. The other servants reported the matter to the master who in his outrage, called the unforgiven servant wicked and had him thrown into jail to be tortured, until he paid back all he owed. Jesus used the story to teach Believers that God will punish those who fail to forgive their fellow human beings who offend them.

> "This is how my heavenly Father will treat each of you unless you forgive your brother or sister from your heart."

Matthew 18:35

The Merciful God does not want any man to perish, his compassion and mercy have no end when it comes to saving the souls of men. The Bible says God's love is steadfast and new every morning, so his redeeming power can never be thwarted by the weakness of human selfishness. The Bible declares God's unfailing love and mercy towards humanity.

> "The steadfast love of the Lord never ceases, his mercies never come to an end, they are new every morning, great is your faithfulness."
>
> Lamentations 3:22-23

Abraham relying on the merciful nature of God interceded to save his nephew Lot and the people of Sodom and Gomorrah from God's wrath and his plan to destroy the city because of their sin.

Abraham's intercession for Sodom and Gomorrah

> "The men turned away and went toward Sodom, but Abraham remained standing before the Lord. Then Abraham approached him and said: Will you sweep away the righteous with the wicked? What if there are fifty righteous people in the city? Will you sweep it away and not spare the place for the sake of the fifty righteous people in it? Far be it from you to do such a thing, to kill the righteous with the wicked, treating the righteous and the wicked alike. Far be

it from you! Will not the judge of all the earth, do, right?"

"The Lord said, if I find fifty righteous people in the city of Sodom, I will spare the whole place for their sake."

Genesis 18:22-26

Moses in his leadership role over a rebellious people of Israel often trusted the merciful nature of God to help the people avert God's vengeance. On an occasion, Moses pleaded with God and said:

Moses' intercession for the Israelites

"Why should the Egyptians speak and say he brought them out to harm them, to kill them in the mountains and to consume them from the face of the earth? Turn from your fierce wrath and from this harm to your people. Remember Abraham, Isaac, and Israel, your servants to whom you swore by yourself. I will make your descendants as many as the stars in the sky and I will give your descendants all this land I promised them, and it will be their inheritance forever."

"Then the Lord relented and did not bring on his people the disaster he had threatened."

Exodus 32:12-14

God listens to intercessory prayers and forgives nations of their sins, so, Christians can therefore, follow the examples of Abraham and Moses' intercession and pray for their nations with intercessory prayers trusting the God of mercy to forgive sins and relent from sending them calamity. The Bible says righteousness exalts a nation, but sin condemns any people (Proverbs 14:34). So, Christians should pray that the people of every nation would pursue righteousness in Christ Jesus.

The parable of the prodigal son is a great illustration of God's forgiving grace. Jesus, in his teaching on the kingdom of God, in the Book of Luke 15:11-32 tells a story about a prodigal son, who demanded his inheritance, left home, and squandered his wealth. But when he became poor and was suffering, he came to his senses and returned to his father's house. The father, an image of God, welcomed his lost son with celebration and restored him to his former glory. The parable shows the Merciful God is willing to forgive and save his people. The father of the prodigal son is a splendid example of God's love, mercy, and forgiveness. God is forever faithful and loyal to those who serve him in spirit and truth.

PRAYER

Our Merciful Father, we thank you for your mercy and grace over Believers all over the world. We ask that you give Christians' the grace to be kind, merciful, compassionate, and gracious. We pray that our nations would pursue righteousness in Jesus' name. Amen.

Chapter 41

Elohim Avraham, Yitzhak V Yaakov - The God of Abraham, Isaac, and Jacob

"God told Moses; say to the Israelites, the Lord of your fathers, the God of Abraham, the God of Isaac and the God of Jacob has sent me to you. This is my name forever and this is how I am to be remembered in every generation."

EXODUS 3:15

Moses asked God for his name at his calling at the burning bush (Exodus 3) where God asked him to go and deliver the Israelites from the bondage of slavery in Egypt. Moses understood human psychology, knowing the fact that human beings are doubters, he knew the Israelites may doubt the existence of a God who can save and deliver them or believe he had been sent by God. This may be due to his previous experience, in his failed attempt to deliver the people from oppression by killing an Egyptian to save an Israelite during a fight (Exodus 2:11-22). The next day, he saw two Hebrew men fighting, he asked the one in the wrong, why he was hitting his fellow Hebrew, but the man said to Moses:

> "Who made you ruler and judge over us? Are you thinking of killing me as you killed an Egyptian? Then Moses was afraid, and thought, what I did must have become known. When Pharoah heard of this, he tried to kill Moses, but Moses fled from Pharoah and went to live in Midian where he sat down by a well."
>
> Exodus 2:14-15

God understood Moses' plight, he gave him his name - the God of Abraham, so, the Israelites may believe he had sent Moses. The name of God - the God of Abraham, Isaac, and Jacob was meant to remind the Israelites of the covenant relationship and the promises of God to their fathers which God declared will endure through all generations.

> "And I will establish my covenant between me and you and your seed after you in their generations for an everlasting covenant to be a God unto you and to your seed after you."
>
> Genesis 17:7-8

The seed of Abraham is anyone and everyone who puts their trust and faith in the Lord Jesus Christ as Lord and Saviour.

"If you belong to Christ, then you are Abraham's seed, and heirs according to the promise."

Galatians 3:29

PRAYER

O Lord, God of Abraham, Isaac, and Jacob, we thank you that you are our God, we pray that you bless Believers with all the promises of life and godliness found in Christ Jesus. Amen.

CHAPTER 42

JEHOVAH MEKADDISHKEM - THE LORD WHO SANCTIFIES

"Tell the Israelites, surely you must keep my Sabbath for this will be a sign between me and you for the generations to come so that you may know that I am the Lord who sanctifies you."

EXODUS 31:13

The word sanctify means to set apart, consecrate, declare something or a person holy for sacred use or assignment. It could also mean purification from sin or cleansing from evil. Sanctification comes by the blood of Jesus Christ, the name of Jesus, the word of God, and by the Holy Spirit. God is Holy, he demands holiness from his people, but he helps them in the process.

"Consecrate yourselves therefore and be holy because I am the Lord your God. And you shall keep my statutes and practice them. I am the Lord who sanctifies you."

Leviticus 20:7-8

Living a sanctified life requires obedience to the word of God.

"To sanctify her, cleansing her by the washing with water through the word."

Ephesians 5:26

Jesus Christ prayed for his disciples, asking God to sanctify them by his word (John 17:17). The blood of Jesus also cleanses people from sin and sanctifies Believers in Christ.

"How much more then will the blood of Christ who through the eternal Spirit offered himself unblemished to God, cleanse our consciences from acts that lead to death, so that we may serve the living God."

Hebrews 9:14

"Jesus also suffered outside the city gate, to make the people holy through his blood."

Hebrews 13:12

The gospel teaches that sanctification is conducted in the name of Jesus and by the spirit of God.

> "And that is what some of you were. But you were washed, sanctified, justified in the name of the Lord Jesus Christ and by the spirit of God."
>
> 1 Corinthians 6:11

The simple step to take towards sanctification is repentance and the confession of sin.

> "If we confess our sins, he is faithful and just and will forgive us our sins and purify us from all unrighteousness."
>
> 1 John 1:9

There is hope for anyone and everyone, who calls on the God of Sanctification. The gospel gives the good news that God will not cast anyone out of his kingdom, who comes to him with a contrite heart. Salvation and Sanctification are given to whoever calls on the name of God. Once justified and sanctified in Christ Jesus, a person becomes a new creation, what Christians call 'Born Again.'

> "Therefore, if anyone is in Christ, the new creation has come, the old has gone, the new is here."
>
> 2 Corinthians 5:17

PRAYER

God of sanctification, we pray that you cleanse us from sin by your truth and spirit. We ask that you call into your kingdom those who do not yet know you as God who sanctifies in Jesus' name. Amen.

Chapter 43

Elohim - The Lord God

"This is the account of the heavens and the earth when they were created in the day the Lord God made them."

GENESIS 2:4

Elohim the Lord God is one of the first names by which God revealed himself to human beings. Elohim means God, meaning the creator and mighty God. God created the heavens and the earth; he showed his infinite wisdom by his creative power.

The gospel preaches the good news that God wants to be the Lord God to everyone and anyone who asks him. God is love, his love is infinite, and he enjoys being the Lord to human beings. His love did not stop at creation, he continues to relate with human beings as their Lord, saviour, and redeemer. It is refreshing to know that God has promised to be with his people as their God until the end of the age.

"Teaching them to observe all things that I have commanded you, and lo, I am with you always, even to the end of the age. Amen."

Matthew 28:20

> ## PRAYER
> *Dear Lord, we thank you for your holy name, Elohim. We thank you for the privilege to call you, LORD in Jesus' name. Amen.*

CHAPTER 44

JEHOVAH ROHI - THE LORD OUR SHEPHERD

"The Lord is my shepherd; I shall not want."

PSALM 23:1

A shepherd is a person who tends and rears sheep. The Bible says God is a good shepherd. God is the shepherd of his people, like every good shepherd, he guides, leads, protects, comforts, and offers direction and provision to those who obey him and do his will. The gentleness and lovingkindness of God are expressed in the name of God our Shepherd.

"He will feed his flock like a shepherd. He will carry the lambs in his arms, holding them close to his heart. He will gently lead the mother sheep with their young."

Isaiah 40:11

Psalm 23 captures the unique role of a shepherd, it gives a full description of the job, listing the responsibilities of a good shepherd.

Psalm 23

"The Lord is my shepherd, I lack nothing. He makes me lie down in green pastures, he leads me beside quiet waters, he refreshes my soul.

He guides me along the right paths for his name's sake. Even though I walk through the darkest valley. I will fear no evil, for you are with me; your rod and your staff, they comfort me. You prepare a table before me in the presence of my enemies. You anoint my head with oil, my cup overflows.

Surely your goodness and love will follow me all the days of my life, and I will dwell in the house of the Lord forever."

Psalm 23:1-6

Psalm 23 describes how well God our Shepherd takes care of his people. The knowledge provided by this name of God, helps Christians appreciate God's benevolent nature. The name provides insight into God's providence. Christians always acknowledge the caring nature of God through the act of praise and thanksgiving expressing their appreciation with the name of God their Shepherd. Jacob at the point of his death blessed his children and acknowledged God as his Shepherd.

> "Then he blessed Joseph and said, may the God before whom my fathers, Abraham and Isaac faithfully walked, the God who has been my Shepherd all my life to this day. The angel who has delivered me from all harm, may he bless these boys. May they be called by my name and the names of my fathers, Abraham and Isaac, and may they increase greatly on the earth."
>
> Genesis 48:15-16

The Bible says God is the Shepherd and Believers are the sheep of his pasture.

> "You are my sheep, the sheep of my pasture, and I am your God, declares the Sovereign Lord."
>
> Ezekiel 34:31

Sheep symbolises obedience and gentleness which informs us that God only leads willing people. The Bible says those who are willing and obedient will eat the good of the land (Isaiah 1:19). Therefore, Christians must obey the word of God and keep his commandments because God cannot lead those who are stubborn and disobedient. The illustration of a sheep (a docile and easy-going animal, who listens to the shepherd's guidance, and follows his lead) is an effective way of God saying to his people to be obedient, otherwise, he cannot be their shepherd.

> "The Israelites are stubborn, like a stubborn heifer. How then can the Lord pasture them like lambs in a pasture."
>
> Hosea 4:16

There is no better way of living the good life than to be obedient and God-fearing, feeding daily on his word, and enjoying the green pasture of God's lush provision and protection. The Bible says God is a good shepherd who sacrifices his own life for the safety and security of his people. Jesus told the people that he is a good shepherd.

JESUS THE GOOD SHEPHERD

> "I am the good shepherd. The good shepherd sacrifices his life for the sheep.
>
> A hired hand will run when he sees a wolf coming. He will abandon the sheep because they don't belong to him, and he isn't their shepherd. And so, the wolf attacks them and scatters the flock.
>
> The hired hand runs away because he is working only for the money and doesn't care about the sheep.
>
> I am the good shepherd, I know my sheep, and they know me"
>
> John 10:11-14

PRAYER

O Lord, our Shepherd, we give you thanks for being a good shepherd. Thank you for your care, provision, protection, and guidance. We praise your holy name in Jesus' name. Amen.

Chapter 45

Jehovah Misgab - The Lord Our High Tower

"The Lord is my rock, my fortress, and my deliverer, my God, my strength in whom I will trust, my buckler and the horn of my salvation and my high tower."

PSALM 18:2

A tower is a big building, usually fortified and used as a military base or a church. The Tower figuratively is a symbol of protection; it means a stronghold or a place of safety. The Bible declares the name of the Lord as a strong tower, where Christians find safety and security.

"The name of the Lord is a strong tower, the righteous runs to it and they are safe."

Proverbs 18:10

We can picture God our High Tower, as a fortified city with high walls, and fortified security gates, where Believers hide and find security and protection from the enemy. God's name is a rock and a fortress, in his name, Believers will find strength and not be susceptible to outside influence or disturbance by the evil one or challenges of life. God's name is their shield and fortress in the day of troubles or tribulation.

> "The Lord is my rock, my fortress, and my deliverer. My God is my rock in whom I take refuge, my shield, and the horn of my salvation. My stronghold, my refuge, and my saviour. You save me from violence."
>
> 2 Samuel 22:2-3

> "Lord, you are my strength and fortress, my refuge in the day of trouble! Nations from around the world will come to you and say, our ancestors left us a foolish heritage, for they worshipped worthless idols."
>
> Jeremiah 16:19

God our High Tower is a refuge of strength and a fortress against the enemy.

> "For you have been my refuge, a tower of strength against the enemy."
>
> Psalm 61:3

The benefit of knowing God as High Tower is peace and freedom from fear. God always encourages his people not to fear the enemy, because he is their High Tower. Faith in God and knowing his name as protector is the Believer's shield against the evil one. Gideon found rest in the name of God - Jehovah Shalom, he praised the Lord who comforted and encouraged him not to fear with the name Jehovah Shalom, The Lord is Peace. Christians must, therefore, overcome fear by putting their trust and hope in their God the High Tower, knowing, and believing God is their strength, and in him there is safety.

> "The Lord is my light and my salvation, whom shall, I fear? The Lord is the strength of my life, whom shall I be afraid of?"
>
> Psalm 27:1

The above scripture is so powerful, it should reassure Christians not to fear because God has not given them a spirit of fear but of power, love, and a sound mind (2 Timothy 1:7). Therefore, whenever Believers become afraid, the name the Lord our High Tower is a useful name to call upon God in prayer.

> "What time I am afraid, I will trust in you."
>
> Psalm 56:3

God our High Tower empowers his people not just to overcome the devil and stay on top of evil, but to also prosper in the presence of enemies (Psalm 23:5).

PRAYER

O Lord our High Tower, our Lord, Saviour, protector, encourager, and the restorer of our soul, we thank you for your loving devotion, in Jesus' name. Amen.

Chapter 46

Adonai - The Lord God

"But Abram said: Sovereign LORD, what can you give me since I remain childless and the one who will inherit my estate is Eliezer of Damascus?"

Genesis 15:2

Adonai is one of the most prominent names of God in the Old Testament. Adonai is a Hebrew word, which translates as Lord in the English Language. A Lord is a person of great wealth, power, and authority. The word Lord also means master, expressing the sovereignty of God. Christians refer to Jesus Christ as Lord. We declare Jesus is Lord, and Jesus confirmed he is indeed Lord.

"You call me Teacher and Lord, rightly so, because I am."

John 13:13

Jesus is Lord because he has power, authority, and superiority over other gods. It takes a personal acceptance and declaration of Jesus Christ as Lord to become a 'Born Again' Christian. The process requires a person to believe Jesus is the Messiah (anointed Son of God) and confess him as their Lord and Saviour. The procedure takes sincere repentance with a contrite heart. The Christian doctrine teaches: Jesus is the Messiah, the Son of God, who manifested in the world and lived in the human body. He died and was resurrected by the power of the Holy Spirit, and in him, Believers receive forgiveness of sin and are saved.

> "If you declare with your mouth, 'Jesus is Lord,' believe in your heart that God raised him from the dead, you will be saved. For it is with your heart that you believe and is justified, and it is with your mouth that you profess your faith and are saved."
>
> Roman 10:9-10

Therefore, making Jesus the Lord and Saviour is a submission of the human will to God's authority. The gospel makes it clear that no one can call Jesus, LORD, except by the revelation of the Holy Spirit. The revelation and faith that Jesus is the Son of God, and confession of sin are the criteria to becoming a child of God. Belief and faith, give a Believer the privilege to call God Father, Master, and Lord.

> "Therefore, I want you to know that no one who is speaking by the Spirit of God says, "Jesus be

cursed," and no one can say, "Jesus is Lord," except by the Holy Spirit."

1 Corinthians 12:3

> ## PRAYER
> *Adonai our Lord, we ask that you reveal yourself to those who do not yet know you as their Messiah, in Jesus' name. Amen.*

CHAPTER 47

EL NAS - THE FORGIVING GOD

"Who is a God like you, who pardons sin and forgives the transgression of the remnant of his inheritance? You do not stay angry forever but delight to show mercy."

MICAH 7:18

El Nas means the Forgiving God. The name describes the compassionate and merciful nature of God (Micah 7:19). God is a loving and merciful God who forgives the sin of the world. God's forgiveness of sin is not earned, it is an unmerited, undeserved sacred grace, given free of charge to humanity. However, Jesus paid the price, through the shedding of his precious blood as the unblemished sacrificial Lamb of God the Father. The sin of disobedience committed by the first man Adam in the Book of Genesis was blotted off-record by the blood of Jesus Christ, the

Son of God. He was crucified for the forgiveness of human beings, so, those who have faith in him can obtain forgiveness of sin, redemption, salvation, and eternal life.

The good news of the Gospel acknowledges the fact that God is not a respecter of persons, he is an inclusive God who extends his forgiveness to everyone. The forgiving God gives his grace and mercy to whoever calls on him and it is this group of people the Bible named Christians or Believers in the Christian Faith. God forgave the sin of the world by giving his only begotten Son, to atone for the sin of all humanity. However, the forgiveness of sins can only be obtained in faith in Jesus Christ the Son of God. The reason being God gave his only begotten Son that whoever believes in him shall not perish but have forgiveness and eternal life.

> "For God so loved the world that he gave his one and only son, that whoever believes in him shall not perish but have eternal life."
>
> John 3:16

The Bible made it clear there is no other name by which human beings can be saved from their sin but Jesus. There is scriptural evidence of the truth that salvation and forgiveness can only occur in Jesus the Son of God.

> "She will give birth to a son, and you are to give him the name Jesus because he will save his people from their sins."
>
> Matthew 1:21

> "Whosoever believes and is baptised will be saved, but whoever does not believe will be condemned".
>
> Mark 16:16

On the day of Pentecost, Peter preached a sermon on the fact that the crucified Jesus was the Messiah in whom humanity can find salvation. The sermon touched the heart of the people, so, everyone asked him what to do to be saved. They repented and those who accepted his message were baptised. About three thousand people were added to the church that day (Acts 2:41). The message was none other than **Jesus is Lord!**

> "Therefore, let all Israel know with certainty that God has made this Jesus whom you crucified, both Lord and Christ! When the people heard this, they were cut to the heart and asked Peter and the other apostles, Brothers, what shall we do? Peter replied, Repent and be baptised, every one of you, in the name of Jesus Christ for the forgiveness of your sins, and you will receive the gift of the Holy Spirit."
>
> Acts 2:36-38

PRAYER

Jehovah El Nas, the Forgiving God, we thank you for your mercy and the forgiveness of sin through your Son Jesus Christ. We declare you Lord and Saviour in Jesus' name. Amen.
JESUS IS LORD!

Chapter 48

Jehovah Makkeh - The Lord Who Smites

"And mine eye shall not spare, neither will I have pity: I will recompense thee according to thy ways and thine abominations that are in the midst of thee, and ye shall know that I am the LORD that smiteth."

EZEKIEL 7:9

Jehovah the Lord who Smites is one of the few names of God that Christians would prefer not to talk about because it instils holy fear in people. However, the fear of God is a great tool for gaining wisdom for living a godly and successful life because it inspires a feeling of awe for God.

"The fear of the Lord is the beginning of wisdom. And the knowledge of the holy one is understanding."

Proverbs 9:10

> "The fear of the Lord leads to life, so that one may sleep satisfied untouched by evil."
>
> Proverbs 19:23

As human beings, knowing the greatness of his power and his ability to punish evil and smite evildoers, keep Believers away from sin and wickedness. The awareness that there are consequences and punishment to sin, dissuade people from disobedience and keep them in awe of the vastness of God.

It is necessary to understand every aspect of God that helps us positively, or impacts us negatively, so, we can live life with wisdom. God is a just and righteous God, so, he will by no means, leave the wicked unpunished. He will judge his people fairly because he is our Judge. God is the Lord of Recompense; he repays and avenges his people.

The name the Lord who Smites is an important one because it gives God the upper hand over the wicked and helps him keep his authority and justice.

> "Maintaining love to thousands, and forgiving wickedness, rebellion, and sin. Yet he does not leave the guilty unpunished, he punishes the children and their children to the third and fourth generation."
>
> Exodus 34:7

To avoid God's wrath, human beings are to repent of sin, and they will have freedom from the curse of the law and those of their ancestors through Christ Jesus.

> "Christ redeemed us from the curse of the law by becoming a curse for us, for it is written: Cursed is everyone who is hung on a tree."
>
> Galatians 3:13

Christians are redeemed from the curse of the law and cannot be judged by sin because in Christ Jesus there is the justification of sin. However, justification requires continuous sanctification because Christians must endeavour to live a holy life, stay on the righteous path of life, and avoid sin.

The Lord who Smites is an awesome God, the Bible says it is a terrible thing to fall into the hands of the living God (Hebrews 10:31). The wrath and judgment of God are dreadful, so it is wise to stay away from evil and wickedness. The account in the Book of Exodus, of the plagues sent to afflict the Egyptians is an excellent example that proves the awesomeness of God.

The Book of Exodus recorded the suffering of the Israelites as slaves in Egypt. God sent Moses to deliver the people from their bondage and take them to their promised land. However, Pharoah the Egyptian king had a hardened heart, he refused to release the people until God proved his power through the plagues that brought havoc to the Egyptians.

The Lord who Smites will deliver the righteous and destroy their enemy. Therefore, if there is any wisdom to learn from this name of God, it is the fact that God will destroy his enemies. He punishes those who become his adversary or enemy of his people. The good news in the name is that God will contend with those who contend with his people, he also destroys and helps Believers win over their opponents. Wow! Aren't you glad that the Lord does not just save his people, but he destroys their enemies? Furthermore, the Lord saves not just his people but says he will save their children too.

> "But this is what the Lord says: Yes, captives will be taken from warriors, and plunder retrieved from the fierce; I will contend with those who contend with you, and your children I will save."
>
> Isaiah 49:25

PRAYER

Jehovah Makkeh, the Lord who smites, we thank you for your saving power from the enemy. We thank you that you contend with those who oppose us and smite our enemies. We ask for victory over Satan and every wickedness in Jesus' Name. Amen.

CHAPTER 49

EL KANNA - THE JEALOUS GOD

"Do not worship any other god, for the Lord whose name is Jealous is a jealous God."

EXODUS 34:14

God El Kanna tells us of the jealous nature of God. However, to understand the Jealous God, it is necessary to know the God kind of jealousy. We must therefore clarify the meaning of jealousy and distinguish between the two forms of jealousy. Jealousy is a feeling of envy, resentment, begrudging, or covetousness towards someone's achievement, possession, or favour. Another definition of jealousy is to be fiercely protective of one's right or possession. This second definition is the God kind of jealousy. God is not envious of humankind, he created them and wished them to have a beautiful life. He is the giver of all things, so, how can he be jealous of humans?

Therefore, Jehovah the Jealous God is merely unwilling to share his love for his people with the devil or other gods. God is fiercely possessive and protective of the people he loves, so, Christians who willingly give their will to God, who choose to love and serve him, must remain loyal, faithful, and steadfast in their relationship with God. God expects a hundred percent Christianity. He proved his case through prophet Hosea, asking him to take a harlot as his wife to experience the pain of infidelity that God feels over his people's unfaithfulness to him by their idolatry. Hosea obeyed God and took a prostitute called Gomer as a wife and had sons by her.

> "When the Lord first began speaking to Israel through Hosea, he said to him; Go and marry a prostitute, so that some of her children will be conceived in prostitution. This will illustrate how Israel has acted like a prostitute by turning against the Lord and worshipping other gods."
>
> Hosea 1:2

The Bible tells the account of great leaders who taught the people they lead, the importance of showing God love and loyalty. Joshua challenged the people of Israel, asking them to choose the God whom they want to serve.

> "And if it seems evil to you to serve the Lord, choose for yourselves this day whom you will serve, whether the gods which your father served that were on the other side of the river or the gods of Amorites in

whose land you dwell. But as for me and my house, we will serve the Lord."

> Joshua 24:15

The Living God gives his people blessings and brings destruction upon the wicked. The main message of scripture is to love and serve God alone because he will not share his people with other gods. The relationship with God demands a firm choice. You are either for God or against him.

> "Whosoever is not with me is against me, and whosoever does not gather with me scatters."
>
> Matthew 12:30

Believers, can you watch yourself as you do life daily, are you loyal to God? Or do you mix the simple message of the gospel with idolatry? The gospel preaches good news, it teaches, reproofs, and corrects the people of God. Therefore, this book does not bring condemnation because there is no condemnation in Christ Jesus (Romans 8:1). It is a reminder that the Christian doctrine must be practised solely without idolatry.

> "All Scripture is inspired by God and is useful to teach us what is true and to make us realize what is wrong in our lives. It corrects us when we are wrong and teaches us to do what is right."
>
> 2 Timothy 3:16

Choosing God means choosing obedience to his statutes documented in the word of God, the Bible. The people of God must develop the habit of reading and meditating on the word, as God advised Joshua to succeed in life (Joshua 1:18). Joshua applied God's counsel in his leadership and instructed the people of Israel to keep God's commandment.

> "So, the people said to Joshua, we will serve the Lord our God and obey his voice. On that day, Joshua made a covenant for the people, and there at Shechem, he set up for them a statute and ordinance."
>
> Joshua 24:24-25

Prophet Elijah in the Book of Kings was angry with the infidelity of the people and asked them to choose between God and Baal.

> "So, Ahab summoned all the Israelites and assembled the prophets on Mount Carmel. Then Elijah approached all the people and said: "How long will you waver between two opinions? If the Lord is God follow him. But if Baal is God, then follow him. But the people did not answer a word."
>
> 1 Kings 18:20-21

The Bible made it clear that no one can serve two masters. We must be faithful servants of God.

> "No one can serve two masters. Either he hates one and loves the other or he is devoted to one and

despises the other. You cannot serve both God and money."

Matthew 6:24

Whilst the preceding scripture seems to refer to the god of mammon (money, greed, and avarice) it is an illustration of the fact that the people of God, cannot serve both the living God and idols. God despises the double-minded, so, take a firm decision on whom to worship – God, or the Devil!

> "The double-minded I despise, but your law I love."

Psalm 119:113

Surely, there is no other god comparable to the Living God! The Bible says there is none beside him, nor is there any rock like our God (1 Samuel 2:2). So, why choose idols over him? Why combine God with Idols? There is no God as great and trustworthy as our God the Jealous God, who cares enough for his people to watch over them jealously.

> "What good is an idol carved by man or a cast image that deceives you? How foolish to trust in your creation, a god that cannot even talk!"

Habakkuk 2:18

> "I am the LORD, and there is no other God. I have equipped you for battle though you don't even know me."

Isaiah 45:5

PRAYER

Dear Lord, El Kanna, the Jealous God, we thank you for loving your people enough, to be unwilling to share them with other gods. We pray that you grant Christians the grace to be faithful and steadfast in their walk with you in Jesus' name. Amen.

Chapter 50

Yahweh - The Lord

"I appeared to Abraham, to Isaac and Jacob as El Shaddai - God Almighty, but I did not reveal my name, Yahweh, to them."

Exodus 6:3

God revealed his name, Yahweh, to Moses during his divine encounter at the burning bush, when God instructed him to free the Israelites from slavery in Egypt. Yahweh is translated in the English Language as the Lord. The name is believed to be built on God's name I AM Who I AM. It is one of God's earlier powerful names believed by the Jewish to be too sacred to be spoken or written. It is a powerful and holy name that people hold in awe with a feeling of reverential respect mixed with fear and wonder.

However, as Judaism expanded, Yahweh was changed to a common Hebrew noun, Elohim, meaning God. The purpose was to prove the universal sovereignty of the God of Israel over all other gods. The name Elohim also became too sacred and was changed to the Hebrew name Adonai meaning my Lord. But Latin-speaking Christian scholars eventually replaced the name with Jehovah, meaning the Lord. God's name Yahweh is to be adored and praised.

> "Praise Jah! Praise the name Yahweh! Praise him, you servants of Yahweh, you who stand in the house of Yahweh, in the courts of our God's house."

Psalm 135:1-2

PRAYER

O Lord God, we thank you that you reign supreme on earth, we ask that you be the Lord of our lives in Jesus' name. Amen.

Chapter 51

Jehovah - The Lord

"That men may know that thou whose name alone is Jehovah, art the Most-High over all the earth."

PSALM 83:18

Jehovah means the Lord. It is the Latinisation of the Hebrew name Yahweh which means Lord. The later generation of Christians adopted the name Jehovah as a common name for God. Jehovah is the Highest God, the God of Israel. He wants to be the Lord of all of humankind. He is the Almighty God in whom all creation find solace.

Moses, whenever overwhelmed by his duties as the leader of the rebellious people of Israel, often go to the Lord Jehovah for comfort and guidance. A notable example of such occasions was when the Israelites had no water to drink when they camped at Rephidim during their journey through the wilderness to their promised land. They grumbled and quarrelled with Moses who took the matter to the Lord – Jehovah.

The Names of God

> "And Moses cried unto Jehovah, saying, what shall I do unto this people? They are almost ready to stone me."
>
> Exodus 17:4

The Lord answered Moses and showed him a rock at Horeb which he was to strike with his rod to give water to the people. The Lord Jehovah is a provider and like the name El Shaddai - Almighty God, he gives food, water, and protection to his people. On another occasion, Jehovah supplied the Israelites with food which they called Manna and Quail (supernatural bread and meat from heaven) when they were hungry in the wilderness.

> "And Jehovah spoke to Moses saying, I have heard the grumblings of the sons of Israel, speak to them saying, at twilight, you shall eat meat, and, in the morning, you shall be filled with bread, and you shall know that I am the LORD your God."
>
> Exodus 16:11-12

PRAYER

Jehovah our Lord, we give you thanks that you are our God, we thank you that you are the sovereign God. Help us to acknowledge you daily in our lives as our Lord and provider in Jesus' name. Amen.

Chapter 52

El Ashiyb - The Lord Our Restorer

"When the Lord restored the fortunes of Zion, we were like those who dreamed, our mouth, was filled with laughter, our tongues with songs of joy. Then, it was said among the nations: The Lord has done wonderful things for them."

PSALM 126:1-2

Restoration is the act of returning something to a former owner, place, or condition. It usually means one has suffered a loss or hardship. God is the Lord of Recompense; he repays his people with double blessing for their trouble. God usually restores things to a state that surpasses the former state. He gives compensation and replaces losses; he restores the lives of individual and that of nations.

"I will restore to you the years that the swarming locust has eaten, the grasshopper, the destroyer and the cutter, my great army which I sent among you. You shall eat surplus and be satisfied and praise the name of the Lord your God who has dealt wondrously with you. And my people shall never again be put to shame."

Joel 2:25-26

"Then if my people who are called by my name will humble themselves and pray and seek my face and turn from their wicked ways, I will hear from heaven and will forgive their sins and restore their land."

2 Chronicles 7:14

God restores the lives of individuals who know him. There are notable examples of restored lives in the Bible which proves the fact that God is a restorer. The Bible book of Ruth tells of the wonderful story of the restoration of a Moabite woman called Ruth and her Israelite mother-in-law, Naomi. Both women lost their husbands and possession in Moab, a foreign land, where Naomi and her late husband Elimelech, migrated to escape the famine in Judah.

Naomi decided to return to her homeland of Israel and Ruth came with her. On their return to Israel, they found favour with Boaz, Naomi's late husband's relative. Boaz, a reputable, and rich landowner became Naomi's kinsman-redeemer. He married Ruth who gave birth to a son named Obed. The lives of Ruth and her mother-in-law were transformed for good, both women, became prosperous and happy.

> "He shall be to you, a restorer of life and a nourisher of your old age, for your daughter-in-law who loves you, who is more to you than seven sons, has given birth to him."
>
> Ruth 4:15

Ruth became the great-grandmother of David, through the birth of her son Obed, who became the father of Jesse, the father of King David. She is listed in the genealogy of Jesus Christ recorded in the Gospel books of Luke and Matthew (Luke 3:32 and Matthew 1:5). What a great restoration and miracle! Ruth was a foreigner, not only that, but she was also a Moabite and according to Mosaic Hebrew law, the Israelites are forbidden under the law to associate with the people of Moab (Deuteronomy 7:3). However, Ruth became an exception to the rule, she appeared in the lineage of Jesus, because of her faith in God. When asked to return to her homeland, she replied to Naomi:

> "Don't ask me to leave you and turn back. Wherever you go, I will go, wherever you live, I will live. Your people will be my people, and your God will be my God."
>
> Ruth 1:16

God our restorer, restores lost fortunes. The story of the testing and restoration of a man called Job in the Bible further illustrates the fact that God restores fortunes to his people. The devil made a false accusation against Job, claiming Job loved and feared God because God prospered and built a hedge of protection around him.

"Have you not put a hedge around him and his household and everything he has? You have blessed the work of his hands so that his flocks and herds are spread throughout the land."

Job 1:10

God granted the devil permission to evaluate Job's faith and loyalty, so, the Devil destroyed his possession, children, and health. However, Job remained steadfast in his love for God. He did not deny, or curse God as the Devil expected. As a reward, God gave him a double blessing and restored everything he lost in multiple folds (Multiple Fold Blessing). Simply put, Job gained big momentum and restoration. God restored his fortune, his later years became great, he had more sheep, more sons, and daughters. Therefore, the Book of Job in the Bible declared the later years of Job as greater than his former years.

"After Job had prayed for his friends, the Lord restored his prosperity and doubled his former possessions."

Job 42:10

"So, the Lord blessed Job in the second half of his life even more than in the beginning. For now, he had 14,000 sheep, 6,000 camels, 1,000 teams of oxen, and 1,000 female donkeys. He also gave Job seven more sons and three more daughters."

Job 42:12-13

Jehovah El Ashiyb multiplies whatever he restores, he ensures the glory of the latter is greater than the former.

> "The glory of this present house will be greater than the glory of the former house; says the Lord Almighty. And in this place, I will grant peace, declares the Lord Almighty."
>
> Haggai 2:9

> "Return to your fortress, you prisoners of hope, even now, I will announce that I will restore twice as much to you."
>
> Zachariah 9:12

Job's endurance teaches the importance of Christians exhibiting the fruit of the Holy Spirit – patience and longsuffering, in dealing with trials and tribulation. The Gospel teaches God comforts and restores suffering Christians.

> "And after you have suffered a little while, the God of all grace, who has called you to eternal glory in Christ, will himself restore, confirm, strengthen and establish you."
>
> 1 Peter 5:10

God is a God of restoration; he restores the soul and gives Believers times of refreshing (Acts 3:20). David cried to him when he committed adultery and murder asking for restoration of the joy of his salvation.

> "Restore to me, the joy of your salvation, and uphold me with a willing spirit."
>
> Psalm 51:12

In addition to the refreshing of the soul, God restores the health of his people and grants Believers divine health.

> "But I will restore you to health, and heal your wounds, declares the Lord, because you are called an outcast, Zion for whom no one cares."
>
> Jeremiah 30:17

Whenever the enemy attacks and destroys the possession of the people of God, the Lord of Restoration steps in to deliver his people and give them victory, overflowing joy, and double blessing for their loss. God restores lost glory and gives his people beauty and splendour in place of their shame.

> "Instead of your shame, you will receive a double part, and instead of disgrace, you will rejoice in your inheritance. And so, you will inherit a double part in your land, and everlasting joy will be yours."
>
> Isaiah 61:7

Restoration is refreshing, it brings joy to people's souls. The Bible records how the Israelites were full of joy when God restored them to their land from captivity (Psalm 126). The Lord the Restorer proves the benevolent and caring nature of God. He is Almighty God, El Shaddai, a loving Father who nourishes his people and takes care of them.

PRAYER

Restore us, O God our restorer, make your face shine on us, that we may be saved in Jesus' name (Psalm 80:3). Amen.

Chapter 53

Jehovah Pelet - The Lord Our Deliverer

"The Lord is my rock, my fortress and my deliverer, my God is my rock, in whom I take refuge, my shield and the horn of my salvation, my stronghold. I called to the Lord, who is worthy of praise, and I have been saved from my enemies."

PSALM 18:2-3

A deliverer is a person who rescues from harm or danger. In Christianity, Jehovah Pelet is the Lord the Deliverer. God Almighty gave his only son to atone for the sin of humanity. Jesus Christ the Son of God laid his life down to die on the cross. He rose from the dead and is seated at the right hand of God, interceding for his people. His death was the payment for the disobedience of the first man Adam, which led to the curse of spiritual damnation and death.

The shedding of the blood of Jesus Christ the Son of God, paid the cost for justification granted to those who believe. The Lord our Deliverer saves his people from sin and gives salvation and eternal life.

> "But now that you have been set free from sin and have become slaves of God, the benefits you reap lead to holiness and the result is eternal life.
>
> For the wages of sin is death, but the gift of God is eternal life in Christ Jesus our Lord."
>
> Romans 6:22-23

The Lord the Deliverer, in addition to the gift of eternal life, offers deliverance from the powers of the evil one. God the Deliverer, delivers and saves his people from the powers of darkness, enemies, forces of hell, curses of the law (poverty, sickness, mental oppression), and trials and tribulations.

> "Therefore, let all the godly pray to you while you may be found. Surely when great waters rise, they will not come near. You are my hiding place. You protect me from trouble. You surround me with the song of deliverance. I will instruct you and teach you the way you should go. I will counsel and watch over you."
>
> Psalm 32:6-8

The Lord our Deliverer delivers his people from sin and afflictions. Jesus cast out devils from the people and delivered them from evil spirits. A demon-possessed man at Gerasenes opposite Galilee was set free from the demons that afflicted his mind (Luke 8:26-39). Believers have the power and authority in Christ Jesus to also cast out demons using the gift of discerning of spirit, given by God the Holy Spirit. Jesus Christ the Deliverer declares all authority has been given to him, this power and authority have been passed on to those who believe in him.

> "Then Jesus came to them and said: All authority in heaven and on earth has been given to me."
>
> Matthew 28:18

> "And these signs shall follow them that believe, in my name they shall cast out devils, they will speak in new tongues."
>
> Mark 16:17

Evil spirits can occupy the spirit of human beings including Christians and cause torments and sorrows of the body and mind. Demon possessions can cause illnesses, bondage, and mental health problems. God the Deliverer cast out unwanted evil spirits from his people. However, it is important to note that not all illnesses or problems happen because of demons. There are medical and natural causes that may give rise to illnesses. Christians practising deliverance and the casting out of devils must therefore depend on the leading of God the Holy Spirit and the gift of discerning of spirit in deliverance ministration.

God has given the keys to the kingdom to those who have faith in Christ Jesus. Believers have the authority to command demons to leave the people of God and to set the captives and the oppressed free in Jesus' name. God the Deliverer gives Christians power and authority to forbid or allow things on earth. The Bible confirms Believers have authority over the devil especially when we agree with other Believers in prayer of agreement.

> "Truly I tell you, whatever you bind on earth will be bound in heaven, and whatever you loose on earth will be loosed in heaven. Again, truly I tell you that if two of you on earth agree about anything they ask for, it will be done for them by my Father in heaven."
>
> Matthew 18:18-19

> "And I will give you the keys of the kingdom of heaven. Whatever you forbid on earth will be forbidden in heaven, and whatever you permit on earth will be permitted in heaven."
>
> Matthew 16:19

Whenever Believers pray or administer deliverance to one another, they speak words of affirmation and authority over Satan in Jesus' name as prayer for deliverance.

Prayer for Deliverance (Writer's Version)

"O Lord our deliverer, your word says, whatever, we bind on earth is bound in heaven and whatever we loose on earth is loosed in heaven, therefore, Satan, I bind you in the name of the Father, the Son and the Holy Spirit. Loose this person and go in Jesus' name. Amen"

The Bible tells the story of a woman, who had a spirit of infirmity for eighteen years (Luke 13). She was deformed, with her back bent, so, she could not lift herself. When Jesus saw her, he had compassion for her, he called her to him and healed her, speaking these words: "Woman, thou art loosed from your infirmity" (Luke 13:12).

Deliverance from sin, sickness, bondage, oppression, depression, poverty, failure, death, evil, demons, spiritual and physical wickedness brings joy and gladness to the soul of the Believer. Whenever, God delivered the people of Israel, they rejoiced and sang a new song in praise to him. When God destroyed the Egyptian armies in the sea whilst they were in pursuit of the Israelites, they rejoiced and sang a new song of praise and adoration.

> "Then Moses and the Israelites sang this song to the Lord. I will sing to the Lord for he is highly exalted. Both horse and the driver he has hurled into the sea."
>
> Exodus 15:1

God Jehovah Pelet is a Believer's hiding place and deliverer; therefore, Christians worship God with songs of deliverance and victory. The Bible records David composed a beautiful song of deliverance to worship and thank God following his deliverance from the hand of his enemies and the hand of King Saul (2 Samuel 22:1-51). The song of praise is particularly useful in times of trouble when Christians need Bible verses to read for the courage to win and overcome their enemies.

Caroline Bimbo Afolalu

David's Song of Praise and Deliverance

David sang to the LORD the words of this song when the LORD delivered him from the hand of all his enemies and the hand of Saul. He said: "The LORD is my rock, my fortress and my deliverer, my God is my rock, in whom I take refuge, my shield and the horn of my salvation. He is my stronghold, my refuge, and my saviour, from violent people you save me. I called to the LORD, who is worthy of praise, and have been saved from my enemies. The waves of death swirled about me; the torrents of destruction overwhelmed me. The cords of the grave coiled around me; the snares of death confronted me. In my distress, I called to the LORD; I called out to my God. From his temple, he heard my voice; my cry came to his ears.

The earth trembled and quaked, the foundations of the heavens shook; they trembled because he was angry. Smoke rose from his nostrils; consuming fire came from his mouth burning coals blazed out of it. He parted the heavens and came down; dark clouds were under his feet. He mounted the cherubim and flew, he soared on the wings of the wind. He made darkness his canopy around him, the dark rain clouds of the sky.

Out of the brightness of his presence bolts of lightning blazed forth.

The LORD thundered from heaven, the voice of the Most-High resounded. He shot his arrows and scattered the enemy, with great bolts of lightning he routed them. The valleys of the sea were exposed, and the foundations of the earth laid bare at the rebuke of the LORD, at the blast of breath from his nostrils. He reached down from on high and took hold of me; he drew me out of deep waters. He rescued me from my powerful enemy, from my foes, who were too strong for me. They confronted me on the day of my disaster, but the LORD was my support.

He brought me out into a spacious place; he rescued me because he delighted in me. The LORD has dealt with me according to my righteousness; according to the cleanness of my hands he has rewarded me. For I have kept the ways of the LORD; I am not guilty of turning from my God. All his laws are before me: I have not turned away from his decrees. I have been blameless before him and have kept me from sin. The LORD has rewarded me according to my righteousness, according to my cleanness in his sight. To the faithful you show yourself faithful, to the blameless you show yourself blameless, to the pure you show yourself pure, but to the devious you show yourself shrewd. You save the humble, but your eyes are on the haughty to bring them low. You, LORD, are my lamp; the LORD turns my darkness into light. With your help I can advance against a troop; with my God I can scale a wall. As for God, his way is perfect:

The Lord's word is flawless; he shields all who take refuge in him.

For who is God besides the Lord? And who is the Rock except for our God? It is God who arms me with strength and keeps my way secure. He makes my feet like the feet of a deer; he causes me to stand on the heights. He trains my hands for battle; my arms can bend a bow of bronze. You make your saving help my shield; your help has made me great.

You provide a broad path for my feet so that my ankles do not give way. I pursued my enemies and crushed them; I did not turn back till they were destroyed. I crushed them completely, and they could not rise; they fell beneath my feet. You armed me with strength for battle; you humbled my adversaries before me. You made my enemies turn their backs in flight, and I destroyed my foes. They cried for help, but there was no one to save them, to the Lord, but he did not answer.

I beat them as fine as the dust of the earth; I pounded and trampled them like mud in the streets. You have delivered me from the attacks of the people; you have preserved me as the head of nations. People I did not know now serve me, foreigners cower before me; as soon as they hear of me, they obey me. They all lose heart; they come trembling from their strongholds. The LORD lives! Praise be to my Rock! Exalted be my God, the Rock, my Saviour! He is the God who avenges me, who puts the nations under me, who sets me free from my enemies. You exalted me above my foes; from a violent man you rescued me. Therefore I will praise you, LORD, among the nations; I will sing the praises of your name. He gives his king great victories; he shows unfailing kindness to his anointed, to David and his descendants forever."

2 Samuel 22:1-51

PRAYER

O Lord, Our Deliverer, we praise your holy name, we ask that you deliver us from the evil one and lead us not into temptation, in Jesus' name. Amen.

Chapter 54

El Achba - The Lord Who Hides

> *"For he will hide me in his shelter in the day of trouble, he will conceal me under the cover of his tent, he will lift me high upon a rock."*
>
> PSALM 27:5

The word hide means to keep out of sight. The God who hides in scriptures can be the God who hides his people from danger or the God who hides from his people. Believers must gain the wisdom on how to relate to the God who hides by understanding these two aspects of God. The first definition says God keeps his people from danger and protects them. Psalm 91 says those who willingly come to God in obedience, he will protect and hide from trouble, diseases, and evil. The second definition says he ignores them, especially when they have sinned.

> "Why do you hide your face and forget our affliction and oppression?"
>
> Psalm 44:24

> "When you spread out your hands in prayer, I will hide my eyes from you, even though you multiply your prayers, I will not listen. Your hands are covered with blood."
>
> Isaiah 1:15

The above scriptures tell us of the side of God's nature which Christians are not too keen on knowing, because people usually like the easy-going and gracious nature of God. However, knowing the God who Hides will help Christians fear God in a good way. It also helps in the sanctification of Believers who should always seek God through repentance and prayers. The Bible says it is the glory of God to conceal a matter, but the glory of kings is to search out a matter (Proverbs 25:2). Therefore, one can say, it is the glory of Believers to pursue and seek God through a passion for Christ and the Holy Spirit! The Bible declares:

> "If you look for me wholeheartedly, you will find me."
>
> Jeremiah 29:13

> "Call to me, and I will answer you and show you great and mighty things, which you do not know."
>
> Jeremiah 33:3

King David called to the Lord who hides in prayer when he sinned, and God confronted him through prophet Nathan (2 Samuel 12). He repented, fasted, and prayed to intercede for God to spare the life of his son born from the sin of adultery. Though the baby died as the penalty for his sin, David obtained God's forgiveness and restoration of his soul. He wrote of his experience in prayer in the Book of Psalms.

David's Prayer of Repentance

> "Do not banish me from your presence, and don't take your Spirit from me. Restore to me the joy of your salvation and make me willing to obey you. Then I will teach your ways to rebels, and they will return to you. Forgive me for shedding blood, O God who saves; then I will joyfully sing of your forgiveness."
>
> Psalm 51:11-14

King Saul, on the other hand, did not seek the Lord who hides, rather, he consulted a medium when the Lord hid from him.

> "The Philistines set up their camp at Shunem, and Saul gathered all the army of Israel and camped at Gilboa. When Saul saw the vast Philistine army, he became frantic with fear. He asked the Lord what he should do but the Lord refused to answer him, either by dreams or by sacred lots or by the prophets.

> Saul then said to his advisers: Find a woman who is a medium, so I can go and ask her what to do."
>
> 1 Samuel 28:4-6

Saul's decision was the wrong way to approach the God who Hides. The Medium conjured the spirit of Samuel, who was dead, he answered and said to Saul; the Lord has left him and has become his enemy. He told him the battle will be lost to the Philistines, and the kingdom has been taken from his hands and given to his neighbour, David.

The results both kings received from God were different because of their different approaches to the God who Hides. King David sought the Lord who hides, found him, and obtained forgiveness and restoration. Meanwhile, King Saul who did not seek the Lord who hides, received condemnation because he lacked humility, courage, persistence, and faith. Knowing God and obtaining his mercy takes humility and persistence with effective prayer. James in his writing in the Book of James confirmed this fact.

> "Therefore, confess your sins to each other and pray for each other so that you may be healed. The earnest prayer of a righteous person has great power and produces wonderful results."
>
> James 5:16

Jesus taught his disciples the importance of persistent prayer and never giving up until results are achieved. He illustrated his point with the parable of a persistent widow and an unjust judge (Luke 18:1-18). In the story, there was a widow who persistently troubled a judge to avenge her on a case until the judge got fed up with her persistence and granted her justice which he had initially refused.

Persistent Prayer Request

> "The judge ignored her for a while, but finally he said to himself, I don't fear God or care about people, but this woman is driving me crazy. I'm going to see that she gets justice because she is wearing me out with her constant requests!
>
> **Then the Lord said**, learn a lesson from this unjust judge. Even he rendered a just decision in the end, so don't you think God will surely give justice to his chosen people who cry out to him day and night? Will he keep putting them off?"
>
> Luke 18:4-7

The lesson for Believers is to be importunate servants of God, to persist in prayer, looking for and pursuing God until he relents, forgives, and restores their soul. He is a forgiving and merciful God, and he will never forsake those who truly call on him.

> "The Lord is righteous in all his ways and kind in all his deeds. The Lord is near to all who call on him in truth. He fulfils the desires of those who fear him. He hears their cry and saves them."
>
> Psalm 145:17-19

Seeking the Lord who hides is worth the effort, because he rewards those who diligently seek him, which simply means to approach God in prayer mixed with faith and persistence. God rewards such people with revelations and insight into wonderous things that he intends to do in their lives, nations, or the world at large. So, Believers need not be anxious but pray without ceasing obtaining the joy of answered prayers and the joy of his presence.

> "Do not be anxious about anything but in every situation, by prayer and petition, with thanksgiving, present your requests to God."
>
> Philippians 4:6

> "Pray continually, give thanks in all circumstances, for this is God's will for you in Christ Jesus."
>
> 1 Thessalonians 5:17-18

> "And without faith, it is impossible to please God, because anyone who comes to him must believe that he exists and that he rewards those who earnestly seek him."
>
> Hebrews 11:6

> "You will show me the way of life, granting me the joy of your presence and the pleasures of living with you forever."
>
> Psalm 16:11

PRAYER

O Lord, give us the grace and courage to remain steadfast in prayer, presenting our prayer requests before you with faith and thanksgiving, in Jesus' name. Amen.

Chapter 55

Jah - Jehovah

*"Sing to God, sing praises to his name,
extol him that rides upon the heavens by
his name Jah and rejoice before him."*

Psalm 68:4

The name of God Jah which is sometimes spelt as YAH means the Lord. The name of God Jehovah God is above every other name. The name Jah expresses the power of God. He has the power to ride upon the heavens. Jah is the shortened version of Jehovah, a Latin version of the name of God Yahweh which means the Lord.

Jah, the Lord God is the creator of heaven and earth. He makes heaven his abode and the earth his footstool.

"This is what the Lord says, heaven is my throne, and the earth is my footstool. Could you build me a temple as good as that? Could you build me such a resting place?"

Isaiah 66:1

He is the creator and the maker of human beings; he is our Lord God.

"He lays the beams of his upper chamber on their waters. He makes the clouds his chariot, and rides on the wings of the wind."

Psalm 104:3

Believers are encouraged to praise and exalt the name of God; the Lord Jah is to be praised!

"Praise ye Jah! For Jehovah is good, sing praise to his name for it is pleasant."

Psalm 135: 3

PRAYER

Jehovah God, we give thanks for your providence and care over the inhabitants of the world. We bless your holy name Jah; may your precious name be blessed forever in Jesus' name. Amen.

Chapter 56

Jehovah Magowr - The Fountain of Living Water

"Jesus answered, if you knew the gift of God, and who is asking you for a drink, you would have asked him, and he would have given you living water."

JOHN 4:10

God is the fountain of living water; this refers to God as the giver of life; the source of our salvation. Jesus revealed himself to the Samaritan woman, whom he met at a well on his journey from Judea to Galilee. When the woman came to draw water from the well, Jesus asked her to give him water to drink. The woman said:

"You are a Jew, and I am a Samaritan, how can you ask me for a drink?"

> "Jesus answered, if you knew the gift of God and who is asking you for a drink, you would have asked him, and he would have given you living water."

John 4:7-10

When Believers accept Jesus as their Lord and saviour, they receive the gift of the Holy Spirit. The Holy Spirit gives the springs of living water, which is the well of salvation accompanied with the fruit of the Holy Spirit's overflowing joy. The Holy Spirit is the source of the living water. Therefore, the Bible declares, those who thirst should come to God the Living Water, to quench their thirst.

> "But whoever drinks the water I give him, will never thirst. Indeed, the water I give them will become in them a spring of water welling up to eternal life."

John 4:14

> "With joy, you will draw water from the spring of salvation."

Isaiah 12:3

> "If anyone is thirsty, let him come to me and drink. Whoever believes in me, as the Scripture has said, streams of living water will flow from within him. He was speaking about the Spirit whom those who believed in him were later to receive. For the Spirit had not yet been given, because Jesus had not yet been glorified."

John 7:37-39

God the Fountain of Living Water is the giver of life, the source of eternal life. Christians, therefore, must stay connected to God to keep the sustenance of his living water. The Israelites often forsake God the Fountain of Living Water, making God angry, resulting in negative consequences.

> "O Lord the hope of Israel, all who forsake you, shall be put to shame; those who turn away from you shall be written in the dust, for they have forsaken the Lord, the fountain of living water."
>
> Jeremiah 17:13

> "Be stunned by this O heaven, be shocked and utterly appalled, declares the Lord, for my people have committed two evils. They have forsaken me; the fountain of living water and they have dug their cisterns, broken cisterns that cannot hold water."
>
> Jeremiah 2:12-13

Believers, therefore, must remain in God to continue to be fruitful and enjoy abundant life.

> "Remain in me, and I will remain in you. For a branch cannot produce fruit if it is severed from the vine, and you cannot be fruitful unless you remain in me."
>
> John 15:4

PRAYER

Lord, the Fountain of Living Water, we thank you for your living water that gives us life in abundance. We ask that you keep us rooted in your word in Jesus' name. Amen.

CHAPTER 57

YESHUA - THE LORD OF SALVATION

"For God so loved the world that he gave his one and only Son, that whoever believes in him shall not perish but have eternal life."

JOHN 3:16

Yeshua is the original Hebrew name of Joshua and Jesus of Nazareth. The name means God saves or the salvation of 0. The Bible says salvation comes from God (Psalm 62:1). When Adam sinned, God gave up his Son Jesus to save the world. Yeshua meaning Jesus, is therefore, the Lord of Salvation. He is the Christian's Saviour and Redeemer and whoever believes in him shall be saved and have everlasting life (John 3:16). Old Testament prophets such as Isaiah and Jeremiah prophesied the coming of Yeshua who will be the saviour of the world.

> "Then Isaiah said, hear now, O house of Israel, is it not enough to try the patience of men? Will you try the patience of my God as well? Therefore, the Lord himself will give you a sign, behold the virgin will be with child and will give birth to a son and will call him Immanuel."
>
> Isaiah 7:14

> "Behold the days are coming, declares the Lord, when I will raise for David a righteous branch and he will reign as king and act wisely and do justice and righteousness in the land. In his days, Judah will be saved, and Israel will dwell securely. And this is his name by which he will be called: The Lord our righteousness"
>
> Jeremiah 23:5-6

The Gospel gives the account that confirms the Lord Jesus was born as prophesied by the prophets. He was born as the saviour of humanity. At the annunciation of the Incarnation, angel Gabriel told the Virgin Mary that she will give birth to the Son of God.

> "She will give birth to a son, and you are to give him the name Jesus because he will save his people from their sins."
>
> Matthew 1:21

Jesus is the Messiah, though the Jews do not recognise him as the promised saviour. However, John the Baptist recognised Jesus as the saviour, the anointed one. The first time he saw Jesus, he exclaimed:

> "Behold the Lamb of God who takes away the sin of the world."
>
> John 1:29

> And again, he saw Jesus passing by and said, "Look the Lamb of God."
>
> John 1:36

Andrew the brother of Peter believed the testimony of John the Baptist about Jesus being the true Messiah, he followed Jesus and became one of his disciples (John 1:41). Andrew testified to others about the sonship of Jesus Christ. He told his brother Peter, that they have found the Messiah, the anointed one. Peter believed Jesus was the Yeshua, the Messiah, the Son of the Living God, who will save the world from their sin. Peter declared so, in his response to Jesus' question of whom the world says he was.

> "You are the Christ the Son of the living God. Jesus replied: Blessed are you Simon the son of Jonah! For this was not revealed to you by flesh and blood but by my Father in heaven."
>
> Matthew 16:16

PRAYER

Yeshua our God of Salvation, we believe you are the Lord who saves the world from sin. We pray for those who do not yet know you as their Lord and Saviour, we ask you to open their eyes of understanding, so, they will know you in Jesus' name. Amen.

CHAPTER 58

MESSIAH - CHRIST THE ANOINTED ONE

"Simon Peter answered, you are the Christ the Son of the living God. Jesus replied: Blessed are you Simon the son of Jonah! For this was not revealed to you by flesh and blood but by my Father in heaven."

MATTHEW 16:16

Messiah means Christ the anointed one. It is another name for Yeshua the Son of the Living God. However, it takes the spirit of God for anyone to receive the revelation that Jesus is indeed the true Messiah who has come into the world in the flesh as the son of God. Prophets in the Old Testament Bible such as Isaiah and Jeremiah prophesied that a son of David would be born, and he will save his people from sin.

The Jewish people are still awaiting the fulfilment of the prophecy. However, Christians believe Jesus has already manifested in the flesh and the prophecy of his birth was fulfilled by the birth of the son of the Virgin Mary. John the Baptist recognised and declared to the world that Jesus is the true Messiah. And because of his testimony, Andrew followed Jesus and became his disciple. Andrew introduced Jesus to his brother Simon Peter who also became the disciple and follower of Christ. When Jesus asked his disciples who the world perceive him to be, Peter answered that he was the Messiah, the anointed one. Jesus replied, only God could reveal such a powerful truth to man. Therefore, the birth and death of the Lord Jesus is the foundation upon which the Christian religion stands. The revelation that he has come in the flesh as the Son of God died and resurrected is the bedrock of the Christian Faith. However, this foundational truth of the Christian religion is difficult for the world to understand because it can only be perceived by the help of the Holy Spirit, not by the human reasoning faculty. The Bible says no one can come to Christ the Messiah unless God first calls them.

> "For no one can come to me, unless the Father who sent me draws them to me, and at the last day I will raise them."
>
> John 6:4

The reason being Satan the god of this world has blinded the mind of the world, from perceiving, believing, and accepting the truth of the Gospel of Salvation. The truth cannot be reasoned but perceived.

> "And if the Good News we preach is hidden behind a veil, it is hidden only from people who are perishing.

Satan, who is the god of this world, has blinded the minds of those who do not believe. They are unable to see the glorious light of the Good News. They do not understand this message about the glory of Christ, who is the exact likeness of God."

2 Corinthians 4:3-4

The Gospel is the Good News that Jesus is the Messiah. The Christian doctrine teaches Jesus Christ has been born to the world and has died to atone for the sin of humanity. Christianity teaches whoever believes this truth in their heart, repents, and confess their sin and the truth that Jesus is the Messiah with their mouth will be saved from death, damnation, and hell. They will obtain eternal life which is available from the shedding of the blood of Jesus Christ. Christians believe Jesus the Messiah is the second Adam who replaced the curse of the law and sin, with the grace of life with God forever, known as eternal life (life after death).

PRAYER

Dear Lord, our Messiah the anointed one, we thank you for your redeeming power. We pray you to call those who do not yet know of your love and saving grace in Jesus' name. Amen.

CHAPTER 59

JESUS - SAVIOUR

"She will give birth to a son, and you are to give him, the name Jesus because he will save his people from their sins."

MATTHEW 1:21

Jesus is the name given to the Messiah (the anointed Christ), the Son of God. The name is derived from the Hebrew name Yeshua meaning to deliver, save or rescue. Jesus is the Greek form of the Hebrew name Joshua which means the Lord saves. The name Jesus is the favourite name of God in the Christian religion, it was revealed to the Virgin Mary by Angel Gabriel at the annunciation (an announcement that someone will be carrying a deity in their womb). His divine purpose was to come to the world to save the lost (people who do not yet know or accept Jesus as their Lord and saviour). Jesus is, therefore, the Lord of Salvation, the saviour of the world.

> "For the Son of Man came to seek and to save the lost."
>
> Luke 19:10

Christians acknowledge the fact that Jesus is the Son of God who was born, crucified, died, and was resurrected to save the lost. Jesus is the name above every other name, the Bible says there is no other name by which humanity can be saved except Jesus Christ. Jesus is, therefore, the Lord and Saviour!

> "There is salvation in no one else! God has given no other name under heaven by which we must be saved."
>
> Acts 4:12

In addition to salvation, Christians believe there is power in the name of Jesus to perform signs and wonders. The apostles performed miracles in the Bible book of Acts, by their faith in the power of the name of Jesus Christ, mixed with their boldness, courage, and the empowerment of the Holy Spirit. When Peter and John (the Apostles), healed the crippled man at the gate called Beautiful, Peter ascribed the reason to the power of Jesus' name. So, in his name, Believers obtain healing, salvation and peace.

> "Through faith in the name of Jesus, this man was healed, and you know how crippled he was before. Faith in Jesus' name has healed him before your very eyes."
>
> Acts 3:16

Finally, the name of Jesus is particularly important for prayer requests. Christians use the name of Jesus in their prayer requests, because Jesus promised the Father will grant any request made in his name. Believers, therefore, end every prayer with "in Jesus' name, Amen" They direct prayers to God the Father in heaven through his Son Jesus Christ. The Bible states Jesus is the mediator and high priest whom Christians trust to deliver their prayers to God the Father. Jesus taught his disciples to ask anything in his name with the promise of answers to every request made in his name.

> "And whatever you ask in my name, that I will do, that Father may be glorified in the Son."
>
> John 14:13

PRAYER

Dear Lord Jesus, we thank you because salvation belongs to you. We believe you are the Messiah. We, therefore, ask you to save and rescue lost souls in Jesus' name. Amen.

Chapter 60

Other Names and Title of Jesus

"Therefore, God exalted him to the highest place and gave him the name that is above every name."

PHILIPPIANS 2:9

There are more names of God the Son, revealed in the New Testament Bible that is not recorded in the Old Testament Bible. Christians, use these names and titles to glorify God in praise, worship, and prayer. Below is a list of notable names and titles of Jesus Christ, popular with Christians.

Son of Man

Son of Man is a name the Bible ascribed to Jesus Christ because he is the Son of God, who was born by a mortal mother, the Virgin Mary. The name describes the mortality of Jesus Christ, who manifested in the flesh and lived amidst humanity as a human being. Jesus addressed himself as the Son of Man.

> "Jesus replied, foxes have dens and birds have nests, but the Son of Man has no place to lay his head."
>
> Luke 9:58

Son of God

The Son of God explains the fact that Jesus was conceived by God, he has an immortal Father, God the Father. The Virgin Mary bore the only begotten Son of God by the immaculate conception (without human sexual intercourse). Jesus is the visible image of the invisible God. During the annunciation of the Incarnation, Angel Gabriel announced the birth of Jesus to the Virgin Mary, declaring God the Holy Spirit will overshadow her and she will become divinely pregnant (immaculate conception) and conceive a son without sin.

> "He will be great and will be called the Son of Most High God."
>
> Luke 1:32

God spoke from heaven, confirming Jesus was his son, during his baptism by John the Baptist in the Jordan River.

> "And a voice from heaven said, this is my Son, whom I love; with him, I am well pleased."
>
> Matthew 3:17

It is worth noting, that even the demons recognise Jesus as the Son of God. When Jesus cast out demons, they fall before him and tremble.

> "You are the Son of God."
>
> Luke 4:41

CHRIST

Christ is a title of Jesus popular with Christians, it means the anointed one. The title comes from the Greek word Christos, a word used to translate the Hebrew name Messiah (anointed person). The disciples of Jesus, believed Jesus was the Messiah, the anointed son of King David, prophesied by the prophets as the saviour of the world.

> "The first thing Andrew did was to find his brother Simon and tell him, we have found the Messiah (that is, the Christ)."
>
> John 1:41

> "Simon Peter answered, you are the Messiah, the son of the living God."
>
> Matthew 16:16

The Mediator

A mediator (a Go-Between) is a person who intervenes between two people who at are variance, to reconcile them. Jesus Christ is a mediator between human beings and God. His aim and purpose were to come to the world to atone for sin with his blood, save humankind from their sin, and reconcile them to God the Father.

> "This is why he is the one who mediates a new covenant between God and people, so, that all who are called can receive the eternal inheritance God promised them.
>
> For Christ died to set them free from the penalty of the sins they had committed under that first covenant."
>
> Hebrews 9:15

High Priest

Jesus is our high priest; he is seated at the right hand of God praying and interceding for his people.

> "For we do not have a high priest who is unable to empathise with our weaknesses, but we have one who has been tempted in every way, just as we are, yet he did not sin."
>
> Hebrews 4:15

THE WAY

Jesus declared to the people that he is the way, the anointed one, chosen by God to fulfil his divine promise to reconcile humanity to God. Jesus is the seed of David; he restores righteousness to the people of God. He presents the way through which all who believe in him will be saved. And he boldly said there is no other way to heaven or God besides him. Jesus is the Way!

> "I am the way, the truth, and the life. No one comes to the father, except through me."
>
> John 14:6

LAMB OF GOD

The title Lamb of God recognises Jesus as the sacrificial lamb of God, killed to take away the sin of humankind. In Jesus, Believers have eternal life and freedom from sin and Satan.

> "Behold the lamb of God who takes away the sin of the world."
>
> John 1:29

LION OF JUDAH

The Lion of Judah is the Jewish symbol of the Israelite tribe of Judah. Jesus' ancestral lineage (family tree) or background is traced to the Israelite tribe of Judah. His ancestor was King David from the tribe of Judah. The title connotes strength, kingship, power, and sovereignty.

> "Weep no more, behold the Lion of the tribe of Judah, the Root of David, has conquered, so that he can open the scroll and its seven seals."
>
> Revelation 5:5

Alpha and Omega

The Alpha and Omega mean the beginning and the end. Alpha denotes a God whose origin is unknown because he is the creator of everything, he existed before anything else existed. He is Omega because he has no end, he is immortal and lives forever (the immortal God).

> "Now to the King eternal, immortal, invisible, the only God, be honour and glory forever and ever. Amen."
>
> 1 Timothy 1:17

> "And he will reign over Jacob's descendants forever; his kingdom will never end."
>
> Luke 1:33

> "I am the Alpha and the Omega, the First and the Last, the Beginning and the End."
>
> Revelation 22:13

Bright and Morning Star

The Book of Revelation reveals God the Son as the Bright and Morning Star. This is because Jesus is a star whose destiny to save humankind shines brightly. The gospel tells us, that a bright star appeared in the eastern sky when Jesus was born. This testimony was given by a group of wise men in the biblical story of the Shepherds referred to as Magi. The Star implies the kingship and divinity of Jesus.

> "After Jesus was born in Bethlehem in Judea, during the time of King Herod, Magi from the east came to Jerusalem and asked, where is the one who has been born king of the Jews? We saw his star when it rose and have come to worship him."
>
> Matthew 2:1-2

Jesus testified to the fact that he is the Bright and Morning Star.

> "I, Jesus, have sent my angel to give you this testimony for the churches. I am the Root and the Offspring of David and the Bright and Morning Star."
>
> Revelation 22:16

The Root of David

Root means family or descendant, so the title The Root of David informs us of the origin of Jesus. He is the son of David because he shares his family heritage with King David as his ancestor. God promised Abraham that his generation will forever be king. Jesus called himself the Root and the offspring of David (Revelation 22:16). The Bible documented his family tree, showing he is from the lineage of David.

> "And this is the genealogy of Jesus the Messiah the son of David, the son of Abraham"
>
> Matthew 1:1

> "Thus, there were fourteen generations in all from Abraham to David, fourteen from David to the exile to Babylon, and fourteen from the exile to the Messiah."
>
> Matthew 1:17

BREAD OF LIFE

Bread of life signifies food and sustenance. Therefore, Jesus being the Bread of Life means he is the giver of life. The gospel teaches, Jesus is Saviour, who gives those who have faith in him, salvation, and eternal life. Jesus stands for the word of God, when he spoke to the devil in the wilderness during his temptation, he said the man should not live by bread alone but on every word that proceeds from the mouth of God (Matthew 4:4). And during the last supper, Jesus shared the Holy Communion with his disciples. He explained to them, that the bread symbolises his body that will be broken to atone for the sin of human beings.

> "And he took bread, gave thanks and broke it, and gave it to them saying, this is my body given for you, do this in remembrance of me."
>
> Luke 22:19

Jesus further declares to the people the significance of his body as the bread of life. He said whosoever believes in him will not perish but will have everlasting life.

> "Then Jesus declared, I am the bread of life. Whoever comes to me will never go hungry and whoever believes in me will never be thirsty."
>
> John 6:35

ADVOCATE

An advocate is a person who argues a case on someone else's behalf, a lawyer, or a spiritual intercessor. Jesus is the advocate for whoever believes in him. He intercedes for the people of God and helps them win over sin and overcome Satan whom the Bible state is the accuser of brethren. So, in Jesus the Advocate, we have salvation, because he defends his people from the accusation of Satan.

> "My dear children, I write this to you so that you will not sin. But if anybody does sin, we have an advocate with the Father - Jesus Christ, the Righteous."
>
> John 2:1

The Bridegroom

The bridegroom refers to Jesus as the husband of the Church. He is the head of the church, and the church is the body of Christ.

> "And Jesus said to them, Can the wedding guests mourn as long as the bridegroom is with them? The days will come when the bridegroom is taken away from them and then they will fast."
>
> Matthew 9:15

The Author and Finisher of Our Faith

The author and finisher of our faith mean Jesus begins and completes everything that concerns his people. He fashions their life and ensures they arrive at their expected end. Jesus helps Believers from start to finish of their divine purpose, perfecting all that pertains to their wellbeing. He is the potter that moulds their destiny.

> "Yet you, LORD, are our Father. We are the clay; you are the potter; we are all the work of your hand."
>
> Isaiah 64:8

> "Looking unto Jesus, the author and finisher of our faith, who for the joy that was set before him endured the cross, despising the shame, and has sat down at the right hand of the throne of God."
>
> Hebrews 12:2

> "Being confident of this very thing, that he who began an excellent work in you will perfect it until the day of Jesus Christ."
>
> Philippians 1:6

PRAYER

May God perfects all that concerns you in Jesus' name

THE CHIEF CORNERSTONE

The Cornerstone is the support of a building upon which other building blocks rest. Jesus is compared to a cornerstone because he is the rock upon which the Christian faith rests. As the chief Cornerstone, Jesus ensures the stability of the entire system of our salvation.

> "Let it be known to all of you and all the people of Israel, by the name of Jesus Christ the Nazarene, whom you crucified, whom God raised from the dead by this name this man stands here before you in good health. He is the stone, which was rejected by you, the builders but which became the chief cornerstone."
>
> Acts 4:10-11

King of Kings and Lord of Lords

The title the King of Kings, and the Lord of Lords simply tells us of the kingship and lordship of Jesus. He is supreme and sovereign, the Jews during his trial, declare Jesus, sarcastically the King of Jews.

> "Above his head, they placed the written charge against him, this is Jesus, the King of Jews."
>
> Matthew 27:37

Jesus was identified as the King of the Jews by the visiting wise men around the time of his birth. They sought him at his birth to pay homage because they saw his star and knew he was the King of Kings.

> "After Jesus was born in Bethlehem in Judea, during the time of King Herod, Magi from the east came to Jerusalem and asked, where is the one who has been born king of the Jews? We saw his star when it rose and have come to worship him."
>
> Matthew 2:1-2

Despite the conflicting opinions of other religions, Christians passionately believe Jesus is the King of Kings and the Lord of Lords, and the Bible boldly declares so.

> "And on his robe and his thigh, he has a name written, KING OF KINGS, AND LORD OF LORDS."
>
> Revelation 19:16

THE RESURRECTION AND THE LIFE

This title represents Jesus as the saviour, through his resurrection Christians have eternal life. The gospel states that Believers will die a physical death but will rise to a spiritual form and live forever with God. There is the promise of the covenant of life, an eternity in Christ Jesus.

> "Jesus said to her, I am the resurrection and the life. The one who believes in me will live, even though they die."
>
> John 11:25

THE WORD

The gospel teaches, Jesus is the Word of God, and the Bible states the Word became flesh and lived in the world.

> "And the Word became flesh and dwelt among us, and we beheld his glory, the glory as of the only begotten of the Father, full of grace and truth."
>
> John 1:14

> "In the beginning was the Word, and the Word was with God, and the Word was God."
>
> John 1:1

The Door

Jesus reveals to the people that he is the door to salvation. A door is an entrance, so he is reiterating the fact that only through him is salvation possible. He is the only way mankind can reconcile with God, the Bible says there is no other way by which humanity can be saved, except through the name of Jesus Christ, the door of hope and salvation.

> "I am the door, if anyone enters by me, he will be saved, and will go in and out and find pasture."
>
> John 10:9

The Truth

Truth means sincerity and the quality of being true. Jesus being the truth signifies the authenticity of the good news, that in him, there is salvation.

> "I am the way the truth and the life. No one comes to the Father, except through me."
>
> John 14:6

Saviour

A Saviour is a person who saves people from harm or danger. In Christianity, Jesus is known as the saviour who died and was resurrected to atone for the sin of humanity. In the Old Testament

Bible, Isaiah and Jeremiah prophesied the fact that a saviour will be born to save the world from sin. The prophecy was fulfilled in the Gospel, in the birth of Jesus in whom Believers now have life and owe their existence.

> "For unto you is born this day in the city of David a Saviour who is Christ the Lord."
>
> Luke 2:11

> "For in him we live and move and exist. As some of your poets have said: We are his offspring."
>
> Acts 17:28

PRAYER

Dear Lord Jesus, we thank you for your wonderful names and titles. We praise you our Lord of Salvation in Jesus' name we pray. Amen.
Jesus is Lord!

Conclusion

Those who know their God will do exploits

"Those who do wickedly against the covenant he shall corrupt with flattery, but the people who know their God shall be strong and carry out great exploits."

DANIEL 11:32

The different names by which God is known in the Scriptures offer in-depth knowledge about God. The truth in his names proves and reveals his nature and character comprehensively. One can rightly conclude that the relationship between mankind and God is based on the revelation of his names. His names are the foundation upon which we know him and build our relationship. The good news is, Christians can receive power from the truth revealed in God's wonderful names. It is amazing and overly exciting to know that knowing God and the power in his names will give Believers the power to act and do exploits. The names give answers and solutions to human needs and the challenges of life.

However, it is important to mention that knowing and praying God's name is not enough. The key is the application of knowledge, which means knowledge mixed with faith, courage, and action. The Believer must apply their knowledge with practical goals and actions (knowledge without action is useless).

The Apostles, armed with the revelation of Jesus as the Messiah, the empowerment of the Holy Spirit, coupled with the use of the power of the name of Jesus, proclaimed the Gospel with confidence, boldness, and demonstration of power. This resulted in the performance of the word of God with the manifestation of miracles that were tangible and visible, so no one could deny their great deeds. Their undeniable performance of miracles in the Book of Acts led to the expansion of the Kingdom of God on earth, and the birth of the Christian religion. Peter following his healing of the disabled man at the beautiful gate preached to the onlooker saying:

> "By faith in the name of Jesus, this man whom you see and know was made strong. It is Jesus' name and the faith that comes through him that has completely healed him as you can see."
>
> Acts 3:16

Following Peter's sermon on the day of Pentecost when the Holy Spirit descended on the people with the evidence of speaking in tongues (unlearned foreign languages), the people were amazed and there was a remarkable success for church growth. The church gained momentum; the Bible recorded three thousand souls (people) were added to the church. So, knowledge of the power of the names of God mixed with faith and action brings the Believer exponential results.

> "Those who accepted his message were baptised, and about three thousand were added to their number that day."
>
> Acts 2:41

The Bible says if God is for us, who can be against us? So, we can be confident in God's support, taking courage in his names. God is always supporting us as our Jehovah Jireh, protecting us as our refuge and strength. We know God as our Jehovah Azar which means the Lord our helper, so, we have knowledge God will help, empower, and make us overcomers, responding to us when we make requests with his names. As Christians, the names of God should be meditated upon, memorised, inscribed in our hearts, and prayed into life situations daily.

Finally, the best wine is kept till the last! The greatest name of God is simply FATHER.

FATHER – OUR FATHER IN HEAVEN

We learn this name from Jesus Christ the Son of God who passionately believes God is his Father and teaches Believers to call God Father in prayer.

> "This, then, is how you should pray: Our Father in heaven, hallowed be your name."
>
> Matthew 6:9

> "But when you pray, go into your room, close the door, and pray to your unseen Father. Then your Father, who sees what is done in secret will reward you."
>
> Matthew 6:6

Jesus performed great and mighty deeds because he dared to call God Father and believed God sent him to the world to save the whole of humankind.

> "For I did not speak on my own, but the Father who sent me commanded me to say all that I have spoken."
>
> John 12:49

Hence, the final challenge to the reader is to dare to call God Father. Christians should encourage one another to pursue an intimate (Father/Son/daughter) relationship with God, then, Believers will be known as great children of the Living God and become great like Jesus.

> "He will be great and will be called the Son of the Highest. The Lord God will give him the throne of his Father David."
>
> Luke 1:32

The greatest good news is the desire of God the Father (the creator of all things) to have an intimate, divine, loving relationship and fellowship with human beings.

The Bible records the friendship between God and Adam, God visited Adam in the cool of the day (Genesis 3:8). God also visited Abraham and ate with him (Genesis 18:8). Jesus called his disciples friends. Great men and women in the scriptures, developed great relationships with God, expressing their thanks and friendship with new names for God in prayer. Believers can develop an intimate relationship with God, who wants their love and friendship.

> "I no longer call you servants because a servant does not know his master's business. Instead, I have called you friends, for everything that I learned from my Father I have made known to you".
>
> John 15:15

God wants nothing more than to love and bless human beings, so, he is willing to bless and treat as friends, whoever reciprocate his love.

> "I thought to myself, I would love to treat you as my children! I wanted nothing more than to give you this beautiful land – the finest possession in the world. I looked forward to your calling me 'Father' and I wanted you never to turn from me."
>
> Jeremiah 3:19

Christians can therefore, become a friend of God by believing in him and loving him wholeheartedly. The Bible states because Abraham believed in God, he was called a friend of God, so, one can rightly say faith in God makes a person become a friend of God.

> "And the scripture was fulfilled which says, Abraham believed God, and it was accounted to him for righteousness. And he was called the friend of God."
>
> James 2:23

HALLELUJAH! Glory to God, God is our Father and friend. The Bible states God has adopted us to sonship through his Son Jesus Christ.

> "The Spirit you received does not make you slaves so that you live in fear again, rather, the Spirit you received brought about your adoption to sonship. And by him, we cry, Abba, Father."
>
> Romans 8:16

PRAYER

The Priestly Blessing

"May the Lord bless you and keep you, the Lord make his face shine upon you, and be gracious to you, the Lord lift his countenance upon you, and give you peace. So, they will put my name on the Israelites, and I will bless them."

Numbers 6:24-27

Altar Call – Call to Salvation

"For God so loved the world that he gave his one and only Son, that whoever believes in him shall not perish but have eternal life."

JOHN 3:16

An altar call is an invitation to those who wish to make new spiritual commitment to Jesus Christ the Saviour and become born again Christian through a prayer of repentance and confession of sin and acceptance of Jesus Christ as their Lord and Saviour.

Prayer of Salvation, Author's Version

If you would like to know Jesus as your saviour and sanctifier, say this prayer:

> "Dear Lord Jesus, I believe in my heart that you are the Messiah, the son of God who has come in the flesh and has lived, died, and resurrected for my sin. I ask for forgiveness of sin in your name, I confess with my mouth that Jesus is Lord. I ask

that you come and dwell in my heart. I ask for the fruit and gift of the Holy Spirit with the evidence of speaking in tongues and the joy of your salvation in Jesus' name. Amen."

Congratulations you are now a Born-Again Christian!

Welcome Letter to new Christians

Hey guys,

Welcome to the Kingdom of God, please know that God loves you and has a plan for your life. Below are a few tips for a successful Christian life.

New Christian To-Do List:

- Do get yourself a Bible to read and study the word of God
- Find a Bible-Believing Church to attend and fellowship for a successful life as newborn-again Christian
- God loves you; He has a plan and a purpose for your life
- Discover and fulfil your purpose, then, have influence and make a difference in the world!

Best wishes in your new Christian walk with God!

> **PRAYER**
>
> *Father Lord, we thank you for the new Christians that has just come into the Kingdom of God. We ask that you walk with them, be with them and help them make progress in their Christian journey in Jesus' name. Amen.*

SONG: I 'M A NEW CREATION - I 'M A BRAND-NEW MAN

I'm a new creation
I'm a brand-new man
Old things are passed away
I am born again
More than a conqueror
That's who I am
I'm a new creation
I'm a brand-new man

Oh, hallelujah He redeemed me
I am born again to win
I thank God He justified me
Of His fullness have we
All received of Him

I've received the Christ of Calvary
I have no sense of sin

We have oneness and a fellowship
Delivered from the authority of sin

God has wrought for me redemption
One that covers every need
Perfectly He's restored our fellowship
With no sense of guilt or memory

Credits
Writer(s): David Ingles
Lyrics powered by www.musixmatch.com

SCRIPTURES FOR NEWBORN AGAIN CHRISTIANS

"Like newborn babies, you must crave pure spiritual milk so that you will grow into full experience of salvation. Cry out for this nourishment."

1 Peter 2:2

"Therefore, if anyone is in Christ, the new creation has come: The old has gone, the new is here!"

2 Corinthians 5:17

"Though you have not seen him, you love him, and even though you do not see him now, you believe in him and are filled with an inexpressible and glorious joy."

1 Peter 1:8

"Therefore, there is now no condemnation for those who are in Christ Jesus."

Romans 8:1

"Because of our faith, Christ has brought us into this place of undeserved privilege, where we now stand, and we confidently and joyfully look forward to sharing God's glory."

Romans 5:2

"No, in all these things we are more than conquerors through him who loved us."

Romans 8:37

Author's Comments

Oluwalana – The Lord Our Way Maker

"So, David went to Baal Perazim and defeated the Philippians there. The Lord did it! David exclaimed. He burst through my enemies like a raging flood! So, he named that place Baal Perazim (which means the Lord who bursts through)."

2 SAMUEL 5:20

The name Oluwalana, is one of God's numerous names in the Yoruba Language of Western Nigerian, West Africa. The Yoruba Christians (Western Nigerians Christians) have a culture that is rich in celebrating God with special names. They have a habit of giving their children names that celebrate God. Some examples are my children's Yoruba names.

- Oluwadamilola which means God has blessed me
- Oluwapelumi – God is with me

- Ifeoluwakitan – The love of God never ceases

I like to share my recent experience with a special Yoruba name of God. During the writing of this book, I felt in my spirit that my path suddenly opened during prayer. So, I praised and celebrated with the name of God in the Yoruba Language, Oluwalana which means the God of Breakthrough, the Lord has opened my path, or the Lord Our Way Maker.

The experience reminded me of the story of how King David was elated and celebrated the God of breakthrough after his sudden defeat of the Philistines (2 Samuel 5). In the Bible story, the Philistines gathered against the Israelites at the Valley of Rephaim. So, David inquired of the Lord whether to attack them, he got God's permission, so, he went to Baal Perazim, and there, he defeated the Philistines. Celebrating his victory, he worshipped and named God, the Lord of Baal Perazim which means the Lord who breakthrough like a breaking flood or water.

As David won victoriously, Believers can also win and be victorious in life using God's name in place of prayer. David inquired of the Lord, and he got God's support and overcame. Believers' heart desires will be granted, when they pray using God's name and delight in his names.

> "Delight yourself in the Lord, and he will give you the desires of your heart."
>
> Psalm 37:4

PRAYER

It is my prayer that as Believers learn to trust the Lord and use his name to celebrate his goodness and pray, God will open their paths and grant them all the desires of their hearts, in Jesus' name. Amen.

About the Author

Caroline Bimbo Afolalu is a Christian, devoted to God and prayers. She has been a Christian since childhood but officially gave her life to the Lord Jesus Christ in the summer of 1986 at a Christian crusade in Akure, Nigeria, West Africa before migrating to the United Kingdom in 1992.

Caroline works as a company director with a demonstrated history of working in the food production industry since 2001. She is the founder and director of Beautiful Foods Ltd the owner of Tabitha's brand of Chin Chin, a West African Nigerian Snack operating in London UK.

Caroline is married to Tunde Afolalu since September 1992, they have, three wonderful and successful children – Adebisi Oluwadamilola, Oluwapelumi, and Ifeoluwakitan Afolalu.

Caroline believes in marketplace ministry. She runs a daily prayer and teaching, YouTube channel (Prayer Nuggets) and Tabitha's Charity with a focus on village women in Nigerian villages, alongside running her food manufacturing business in the United Kingdom.

Caroline would like to simply be known as Mrs Caroline Bimbo Afolalu the great! Achieving greatness in the simplest ways as a daughter, wife, mother, businessperson, and woman of God.

Other Books from the Author

How to Start a Business - A Guide to Starting and Growing a Food Business

Beautiful Foods - The Art of African Catering

Upcoming Books

Wisdom Nuggets from Proverbs

Contact Details

Websites

Work

www.beautifulfoods.co.uk
www.tabithaschinchin.com

Charity

www.prayernuggets.com

Works Cited

The Holy Bible

New International Version, New Living Translation,

English standard version, Berean Study Bible, King James Bible, World English Bible, New American Bible, New King James Version.

Song: I am a new creation: I am a brand-new man

Writer(s): David Ingles
Lyrics powered by www.musixmatch.com

Recommended Resources

The Holy Bible

www.ingramcontent.com/pod-product-compliance
Lightning Source LLC
Chambersburg PA
CBHW071902290426
44110CB00013B/1250